Hiking Maine's 100 Mile Wilderness

Help Us Keep This Guide Up to Date

Every effort has been made by the author and editors to make this guide as accurate and useful as possible. However, many things can change after a guide is published—trails are rerouted, regulations change, techniques evolve, facilities come under new management, etc.

We appreciate hearing from you concerning your experiences with this guide and how you feel it could be improved and kept up to date. While we may not be able to respond to all comments and suggestions, we'll take them to heart and we'll also make certain to share them with the author. Please send your comments and suggestions to the following email address: editorial@GlobePequot.com.

Thanks for your input, and happy trails!

Hiking Maine's 100 Mile Wilderness

A Guide to the Area's Greatest Hiking Adventures

Greg Westrich

FALCONGUIDES

ESSEX, CONNECTICUT

FALCONGUIDES®

An imprint of The Rowman & Littlefield Publishing Group, Inc.
4501 Forbes Blvd., Ste. 200
Lanham, MD 20706
www.rowman.com

Falcon and FalconGuides are registered trademarks and Make Adventure Your Story is a trademark of The Rowman & Littlefield Publishing Group, Inc.

Distributed by NATIONAL BOOK NETWORK

Photos by Greg Westrich
Maps by The Rowman & Littlefield Publishing Group, Inc.

British Library Cataloguing in Publication Information available

Library of Congress Cataloging-in-Publication Data
Names: Westrich, Greg, author.
Title: Hiking Maine's 100 Mile Wilderness : a guide to the area's greatest
   hiking adventures / Greg Westrich.
Other titles: Hiking Maine's Hundred Mile Wilderness
Description: Essex, Connecticut : FalconGuides, [2023] | Includes index. |
   Summary: "A guide to more than forty hikes in Maine's 100 Mile
   Wilderness. Discover the highest waterfall on the entire Appalachian
   Trail, remote mountains like Wadleigh, and one of the largest springs in
   New England. Features detailed maps, hike descriptions, mile-by-mile
   directional cues, and much more"— Provided by publisher.
Identifiers: LCCN 2022050449 (print) | LCCN 2022050450 (ebook) | ISBN
   9781493069712 (paperback) | ISBN 9781493069729 (epub)
Subjects: LCSH: Hiking—Maine—Guidebooks. | Trails—Maine—Guidebooks. |
   Backpacking—Maine—Guidbooks. | Appalachian Trail—Guidbooks. |
   Maine—Guidebooks.
Classification: LCC GV199.42.M2 W468 2023 (print) | LCC GV199.42.M2
   (ebook) | DDC 796.510974104—dc23/eng/20221107
LC record available at https://lccn.loc.gov/2022050449
LC ebook record available at https://lccn.loc.gov/2022050450

♾™ The paper used in this publication meets the minimum requirements of American National Standard for Information Sciences—Permanence of Paper for Printed Library Materials, ANSI/NISO Z39.48-1992.

Contents

Acknowledgments viii
Meet Your Guide ix
Introduction 1
    Wildlife 3
    Bugs 6
    Plant Life 9
    Be Prepared 10
How to Use This Guide 11
Map Legend 18

The Hikes

  1 Debsconeag Ice Caves 21
  2 Horserace Pond 25
  3 Lower Bean Pond and Rainbow Deadwaters 30
  4 Rainbow Stream 34
  5 Debsconeag Backcountry, West Loop 39
  6 Debsconeag Backcountry, East Loop 44
  7 Nesuntabunt Mountain from the North 50
  8 Nesuntabunt Mountain from the South 55
  9 Pollywog Falls and Crescent Pond 59
10 Pollywog Falls and Cliffs 63
11 Wadleigh Mountain from the North 67
12 Wadleigh Mountain from the South 71
13 Musquash Ledges 76
14 Tumbledown Dick Falls via the Appalachian Trail 80
15 Tumbledown Dick Falls via Leavitt Pond 84
16 Turtle Ridge from the West 89
17 Turtle Ridge from the East 95
18 Potaywadjo Ridge 101
19 Little Boardman Mountain 106
20 Gauntlet Falls 110
21 White Cap Mountain via Logan Brook 115
22 White Cap Mountain via White Brook 119
23 Hay Brook Falls 123
24 Number Four Mountain 126
25 Baker Mountain 129
26 Indian Mountain 132
27 Rum Pond Loop 136
28 Hedgehog Mountain 141
29 Shaw Mountain 145
30 Indian Falls 150

31 Little Lyford Ponds.. 154
32 Gulf Hagas from the West.. 158
33 Gulf Hagas from the East 165
34 Henderson Brook 171
35 Chairback Mountain.. 175
36 Third Mountain... 179
37 Indian Pond.. 182
38 West Chairback Pond.. 186
39 Barren Mountain 190
40 Otter Pond 195
41 Slugundy Gorge.. 198
42 Vaughn Stream Falls... 203
43 Big Wilson Cliffs... 208
44 Little Wilson Falls... 213
45 Borestone Mountain 218

Appendix: Great Circle Trail.. 223
Hike Index 227

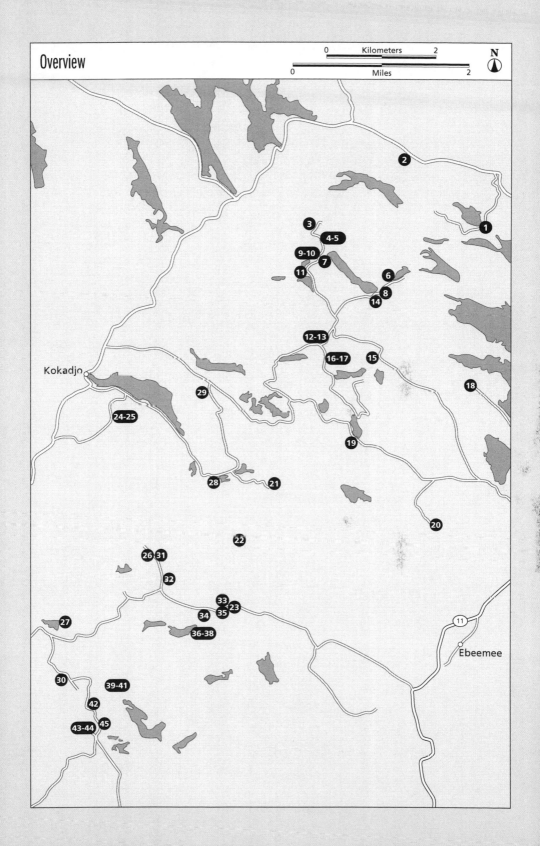

Kokadjo

Ebeemee

Acknowledgments

Hiking is my religion, and the 100 Mile Wilderness is my local church. It's made possible by the tireless work of the volunteers and organizations that work to preserve the 100 Mile Wilderness and its trails. A special shout-out to the Maine Appalachian Trail Club and its section maintainers. Maine is the only state where the AT is maintained entirely by volunteers.

Meet Your Guide

Greg Westrich is the author of seven Maine hiking guides published by Falcon and is currently working on several others. His most recent guides are *Hiking Waterfalls Maine*; *Hiking Maine*, fourth edition; and *Hiking New Hampshire*. Since 2013 he has mapped more than 800 hikes in Maine and 110 in New Hampshire. Greg has also published more than fifty articles and stories in newspapers, anthologies, and magazines, including *Canoe & Kayak*, *BirdWatching*, and *Down East*. He has written about everything from backyard mushrooms to wedding traditions in Aroostook County to coming face-to-face with a bull moose.

Greg earned an MFA in Creative Writing from University of Southern Maine's Stonecoast Program. He teaches English at Deer Isle/Stonington High School. His students call him Mr. Greg and think he's weird because he makes them observe moss up close and read stories about kids who grow wings on their ankles. Greg has also worked as a carpenter, sous-chef in a French restaurant, newspaper carrier, fence installer, stay-at-home parent, children's educational book editor, bookstore manager, and warehouse supervisor in an Alaskan salmon cannery. He spends way too much time thinking about the "nature writing problem." Don't ask him about hiking unless you have a few hours to spare.

He lives in Glenburn, Maine, with his wife, Ann, their two children, and too many pets. He was born in Cincinnati and has visited forty-nine states and most Canadian provinces and territories. Maine is his favorite place, which is why he's lived there for twenty-seven years.

Greg started and maintains the "Wicked Wild 25" hiking list of Maine's wildest hikes. Check out the list's Facebook page for a complete list of hikes and how to earn the badge. Follow Greg's outdoor adventures on Facebook and his website: gregwestrich.com.

Hay Brook Falls

Introduction

On an overcast day in August 1998, my wife and I hitchhiked from Monson village to where the Appalachian Trail (AT) crosses ME 15. We'd spent the previous two weeks hiking the AT from New Hampshire to Monson. We got out of the station wagon and walked across the gravel parking lot under a threatening sky. Next to where the trail entered the woods was a sign reading:

CAUTION
There are no places to obtain
supplies or help until you reach
Abol Bridge—90 miles north
You should not attempt this section
unless you carry a minimum of ten
days' supplies. Do not underestimate
the difficulty of this section.
Good hiking!

The sign at the beginning of the 100 Mile Wilderness

Rainbow Stream Lean-to

Even though this sign has been gone for years, hikers still know to take the 100 Mile Wilderness seriously. Seasoned AT hikers usually spend a zero day or two in Monson resting and eating. And eating some more. My wife and I didn't take any zero days on our hike in the 100 Mile Wilderness, and our physical and mental health suffered for it. The 97 miles from Monson to Abol Bridge (the sign had the mileage wrong) is the longest section on the entire AT without a town or paved road crossing. Thus the name. Over time, the name has come to refer not only to the section of the AT but also to the larger region of mountains and lakes.

It's not a wilderness in the legal sense. The land has been actively logged for generations and is crisscrossed with gravel roads. Even so, the region is wild and remote. There's exactly one hike (Borestone Mountain) in this guide that you reach on a paved, public road. Some of the trailheads are more than 25 miles from the nearest asphalt. There's virtually no cell coverage anywhere in the region except on the highest peaks. Except on the AT itself, you'll rarely see other hikers.

Among AT thru-hikers, the region has a reputation as being flat. It's not. The trail crosses a mountain over 3,500 feet elevation and numerous other small, rugged mountains. In *A Walk in the Woods*, Bill Bryson got separated from his hiking partner their second day in the wilderness on Barren Mountain. When they were reunited the following morning, they gave up and found a ride out on the KI Road, which crosses the region from Greenville to Brownville. My wife and I hiked through in less than six days, but each of us had moments when we were ready to quit. I passed a kidney stone in Gulf Hagas, giving me my trail name. The last afternoon, near the east end of Rainbow Lake, my wife sobbed that she couldn't walk anymore. Dark clouds crowded overhead and thunder rumbled. We had more than 4 miles to hike to reach the nearest lean-to. If there had been a road handy, I think she would have hitchhiked home. In the end, we made it over Rainbow Ledges to the next shelter minutes before the onset of an all-night deluge. Two days later, we climbed Katahdin, completing our twenty-six-day journey. Twenty-six days barely made us thru-hikers, but the thru-hikers who had come all the way from Georgia assured us that Maine was the hardest state. They said we'd earned the title and trail names.

Every year a couple thousand thru-hikers pass through the wilderness on their way to Katahdin. Even more section hikers come just to hike the 100 Mile Wilderness section of the AT. This guide isn't for them. It's for the hikers who want to explore and day hike the larger region. Much of the wilderness is owned by timber companies (about 175,000 acres). They maintain the roads and operate three gates, where you pay a fee to drive their roads, camp at remote sites, and hike. One gate is off ME 11 north of Brownville at Katahdin Iron Works. The second is farther north on ME 11 at Jo-Mary Road. The third gate is on the KI Road east of Greenville. There are two other access points from Kokadjo north of Greenville: Frenchtown Road south of First Roach Pond and Smithtown Road north of the lake. These don't have fee gates. There's also limited access from the south on Mountain Road off Elliotsville Road from Monson. Two of the hikes in this guide are accessed from the Golden Road north of the 100 Mile Wilderness, which you get to from the Baxter Park Road north of Millinocket. In the guide, all driving directions will begin in Brownville, Greenville, Monson, or Millinocket.

The north and western areas of the wilderness are mostly preserves. The Appalachian Mountain Club (AMC) owns about 70,000 acres. Nahmakanta Public Reserved Land is 43,000 acres. And The Nature Conservancy's Debsconeag Lakes Wilderness is 46,000 acres (it's part of a much larger wilderness preserve that extends south and west of Baxter State Park). These are all accessed on the roads mentioned above.

The forty-five hikes in this guide hit the highlights on the AT and across the region. They include the highest peak on the AT between the Bigelows and Katahdin, the highest waterfall on the entire AT, and plenty of trail notorious as roots and rocks held together with mud. The hikes visit more than thirty waterfalls, lots of remote ponds, and more than a dozen peaks.

Wildlife

Many people come to Maine hoping to see a moose. After all, Maine has more moose than any state other than Alaska. You're most likely to see one along the road on the way to the trailhead, but I've seen moose on a number of the hikes included in this

Ring-necked snake

guide. The sound of a rushing stream can hide the sound of an approaching hiker, making a sighting more likely. I once came around a turn in the trail just upstream from Debsconeag Falls and almost walked into a young bull moose. He was hiking down the trail from Fifth Debsconeag Lake to Fourth and I was hiking up the same trail. We were both quite surprised. The moose stood motionless for a moment, then crashed across the stream and up the embankment into the woods.

As you hike, watch for tracks and scat in the trail. Look for moose in shallow water, eating aquatic vegetation. In summer, cows, especially those with a calf, rarely stray far from the water where they feed. Bulls, on the other hand, tend to wander and can be found almost anywhere. Your best chance of seeing a moose on a hike is early in the morning or after sunset. Moose appear to be suffering a serious die-off in Maine right now. Of the calves born in 2021 and tagged by state biologists, 90 percent had died by the spring of 2022. Winter ticks seem to be the primary problem. Many dead moose are emaciated and covered with tens of thousands of ticks. Climate change is a contributing factor.

Spruce grouse

By weight, there are more salamanders in Maine than moose. Which is another way of saying that most wildlife is small. Hiking near water often offers opportunities to see frogs, toads, waterfowl, songbirds, ospreys, eagles, and, yes, salamanders. Don't rush your hike. Take your time and see the woods you're hiking through. You might get lucky and see a porcupine napping in a pine tree, wood frogs congregating in a vernal pool to breed, or evidence that a bear passed through the night before (Maine has more black bears than any other state, but they are very shy).

Many of the forests in the 100 Mile Wilderness are good habitat for grouse and woodcock. Ruffed grouse are common in second-growth hardwoods. The grouse are dependent on the alders and willows there. It's not uncommon in June to be startled by a hen mewling like an injured animal. She's trying to get your attention to lead you away from her chicks. She'll flutter her wings and walk noisily away from you. If you don't follow, she'll sometimes come at you to get your attention. When you see the hen leading you one way, look the other for her fluffy chicks, either on the ground (when very young) or in low, shrubby growth (when older). Spruce grouse tend to be more common at elevation, especially in spruce. My family calls them tree chickens because you can often find them sitting on a low branch, looking like a small, dark chicken. They are not shy and will often strut back and forth across the trail to keep you out of their territory. Woodcock are fairly common but much shyer than grouse. You can often find them in small open patches just as the snow is melting. Otherwise, you're likely to hike right by one without even knowing it.

Bugs

Blackflies are active during the day, especially between Mother's Day and Father's Day; however, in 2022, Maine state biologists announced that blackfly season now lasts all summer. Mosquitoes love cool, damp places, like streams and ponds and dense woods. Some hikers wear bug nets during early summer to ward off the biting hordes. Others dowse themselves with liberal doses of DEET. I prefer to just ignore the bugs or walk faster. You need to find your own comfort level and come prepared to deal with the bugs in your own way.

In the past few years, New Englanders have begun to really worry about ticks. You're most likely to have a problem where the trail passes through tall grass or thick ferns. Some experts suggest wearing long pants tucked into your socks. Personally, I wear shorts and check myself regularly for ticks on my shoes and legs. Since 2013, I've hiked several thousand miles in New England and pulled hundreds of ticks off myself. But I've never had one successfully attach itself to me. There aren't many ticks in the

Family of ducks in Sunrise Pond

Fungus

Blood trillium

100 Mile Wilderness to worry about, but avoid problems by stopping after passing through tick habitat and checking yourself for them. Once you get home, check your whole body. I make it part of my shower routine.

Not all bugs are to be avoided. Maine is home to at least 120 species of butterflies. Many of the showiest are active in habitats you'll be hiking through. We tend to associate butterflies with flowers, but many Maine species don't visit flowers, preferring bare hilltops or piles of bear dung.

Plant Life

When the streams are running high in the spring and the waterfalls are at their peak, the woods are exploding with wildflowers. A succession of flowers bloom until the trees leaf out. The trail descriptions note especially good places to find wildflowers, especially orchids. In the fall, mushrooms erupt beneath forests exploding with color.

The forests of Maine are especially diverse. Maine is the southern extent of many northern species and the northern extent of many southern species. The result is forests with dozens of different kinds of trees. It's also worth noting that Maine is the most forested state in the country. The 100 Mile Wilderness is home to more than fifty species of trees. This diversity is mirrored in the shrubs and herbs found beneath the trees.

Borestone West Peak in winter

Be Prepared

No matter when you hike in Maine, you need to be prepared for the weather to change. In general, wear layers and avoid cotton clothing. Never wear white; it attracts bugs and scares away birds. Keep snacks, water, a flashlight, and a first-aid kit in your pack. Always bring your rain gear. Even a short hike can turn epic if you don't dress and pack smart. With the right gear and clothes, even a dreary day can be a great one in the woods. If you choose to hike in winter—which can be very rewarding—make sure you have the right footwear and layers. Depending on the location and conditions, you may need snowshoes or spikes. Always remember that the 100 Mile Wilderness is remote and mostly lacks cell coverage. On a hike in this guide, you're mostly on your own.

How to Use This Guide

Throughout this guide, the Appalachian Trail is simply referred to as the AT. In the 100 Mile Wilderness, the AT trends northeast but makes a big loop to the east and then back west before heading east across Rainbow Ledges to Abol Bridge. As a result, you can actually be hiking in any direction while hiking northbound. I use northbound and southbound as directions on the AT rather than the actual direction you're hiking.

Each hike begins with a few sentences that briefly describe the hike. Next you'll find the nitty-gritty details.

Start lets you know where the trailhead is. Sometimes the trail is unmarked or confusing. This should clear things up.

Elevation gain gives you a rough idea of how much work it'll be. For every hike, I use gross elevation gain. If a hike goes up 100 feet, down 50 feet, then up another 100 feet. The net gain is 150 feet, but you climbed 200, so that's the number I use.

Distance tells you how far the entire hike is and whether it's an out-and-back, a loop, or a lollipop.

Hiking time is my best guess as to how long the average person will take to complete the hike. This number is mostly for comparing hikes, not a judgment on how fast or slow you walk.

Difficulty lets you know how hard the hike is. Easy hikes have little climbing, are short, and require no route-finding skills. Moderate hikes are more than 4 miles, require some scrambling, or have short, steep climbs. Strenuous hikes are longer than 6 miles, require climbing or scrambling, and involve bushwhacking or using rough, unmarked trails.

Season lets you know when it's best to go. Sometimes access is limited and influences the season. Many of the logging roads used to reach trailheads are not plowed in winter, and those that are plowed are often sketchy. Very few of the hikes in this guide are accessible by car once the ground becomes snow-covered. If you can drive to a hike's trailhead in winter, I note that. Similarly, many of the logging roads are either closed or a mess during mud season. Usually the roads get regraded as soon as they dry out. That doesn't mean you can't get to the trailheads in spring. It just means you need to drive slower and be prepared for rougher conditions.

Trail surface lets you know what the path is going to be like.

Land status lets you know who owns the property and whether it's a park or preserve.

Nearest town gives you the town closest to the trailhead.

Other users is included mostly to let you know whether hunting is allowed in the area of the hike.

Water availability is a part of every hike, but it's not all good for drinking. Any water taken from a stream or pond should be treated or filtered. I try to always mention springs on or near the hikes.

AT through mossy spruce forest

The slide on the hike to Vaughn Stream Falls

Canine compatibility lets you know if dogs are welcome and whether they need to be leashed. Even where there are no rules regarding dogs, please be respectful of other hikers. Not everyone likes dogs, and some people are afraid of them. Those people deserve to hike too.

Fees and permits lets you know if there are entrance, parking, or other fees required to get to the hike.

Maps. Even though this guide includes an adequate map for each hike, some folks like more. I've listed the map number in *DeLorme: Maine Atlas & Gazetteer* and the United States Geological Survey (USGS) 1:24,000 topo for each hike.

Trail contact information is included, even though this guide should include everything you need to hike. For folks interested in camping and other activities not included in this guide, it can be helpful to know where to find such information.

Ice-covered blossoms

Amenities available lists things other than a trailhead and parking area near each trail. In this guide, there aren't many signs of civilization near the hikes. But many of the trailheads have an outhouse, and several are near AMC lodges with amenities.

Maximum grade lets you know just how steep the hike gets and if there's any rock scrambling involved. Used with elevation gain and distance, this gives you a pretty good picture of what you're in for.

Cell service in the 100 Mile Wilderness is almost nonexistent, but you can often get a signal on open ledges and mountaintops. A few of the hikes closer to Greenville and Monson have better coverage. In general, don't count on getting any cell signal while hiking.

Finding the trailhead gives specific mile-by-mile directions to the trailhead from a nearby town or highway junction. When the trailhead and parking are poorly marked—or not marked at all—it will be noted in the directions. Getting to almost all the trailheads in this book requires driving on private logging roads. Conditions vary from season to season and year to year. I drove to most of these hikes in a Honda Fit and the rougher roads with a Honda CRV. If the road is a problem, I'll note that. Each description also lists the GPS coordinates for the trailhead.

There's always time for play.

The Hike is the text version of the specs listed above. I try to include information that will add to your experience while hiking by answering the questions most hikers have. In my years of hiking and writing, I've accumulated dozens of guides and science books. I'm a writer, not a biologist or geologist, but I try to give useful information about what you'll see and where you'll walk.

The 100 Mile Wilderness is geologically complex. Roughly speaking, the bedrock in the southern and western parts is mostly slate; the northern and eastern parts are granite associated with the Katahdin massif. When relevant, a hike's description will explain what the bedrock is and how that impacts your hiking experience.

People tend to think of the northern forest as being primarily spruce and white pine, but most of the lowlands in the 100 Mile Wilderness is blanketed with hardwoods. There's a lot of maple and beech. These often make for vistas with spectacular fall colors and are noted in the description. There's nothing quite like hiking through a beech forest in the fall. The yellow leaves make the very air around you seem to glow. Evergreens don't change color in the fall, but they present various shades of green every spring as new growth pops on each twig. At the same time, every hardwood leafs out at a slightly different rate, showing different colors as they bloom and then leaf out. The spring colors aren't as dramatic as those in the fall but they are still worth your attention. Usually the roads dry up about the same time the maples bloom and this process begins.

The descriptions point out the best places to find wildlife, especially moose and loons. Most wildlife is seasonal and variable. The best ways to be sure to see wildlife are to spend a lot of time in the woods, do it quietly, and do it early in the morning or at dusk. I try to be just as excited about seeing a flock of ebony jewelwing damselflies or a pair of ring-necked ducks as a moose.

Many of the hikes involve mountaintop or ledge vistas. In the descriptions, I try to explain what you're seeing in the distance. I like to stand on an overlook and tick off in my head the names of all the ponds and mountains I can see. The descriptions may not be that exhaustive, but I give you the highlights. I especially mention if you have a view of Katahdin or can see distant mountains outside the region, such as the Bigelows.

I have a particular fascination with peat bogs and their plant life. Whenever a hike passes one, I'll point it out and mention any carnivorous plants you might see. The same goes for blueberries. Hiking along, snacking on blueberries or huckleberries plucked from beside the trail, is one of the great joys of being in Maine.

The 100 Mile Wilderness has a long history of human use—beginning with the Native Americans who occupied the area as soon as the glaciers retreated, through modern Penobscots and Euro-American loggers and adventurers, to us. I try to include relevant history to deepen your experience. The region is a reminder both that it's all land stolen from native peoples (in this case, Penobscots) and that wilderness is more a relationship with the land than the land's state of being.

In the end, I try to describe each hike in a way that enhances the process of completing it. Short videos of many of the hikes are available on my Facebook page.

Miles and Directions: If the description helps you see and enjoy the process of walking, this section makes sure you don't get lost or miss any highlights. This section is especially important for hikes that involve bushwhacking, use rarely-hiked trails, or cross abandoned logging roads and twitch trails. Blazes can be an important tool to keep you hiking in the right direction. The AT is blazed white and well-marked. Other trails are generally blazed pale blue. The AMC has begun blazing its trails with colored plastic diamonds.

Map Legend

Municipal

‒‒‒‒‒ Paved Road

= = = = Unpaved Road

Trails

▬▬▬▬▬ Featured Trail

- - - - - Trail or Fire Road

Water Features

Body of Water

Marsh/Swamp

River/Creek

Intermittent Stream

Waterfall

Spring

Symbols

∩ Arch

▲ Backcountry campsite

≍ Bridge

■ Building/Point of Interest

▲ Campground

× Elevation

•—• Gate

▲ Mountain/Peak

🅿 Parking

🔆 Scenic View/Overlook

○ Towns and Cities

❶ Trailhead

Trail beneath the cliffs on Turtle Ridge

A hiker climbs out of an ice cave.

1 Debsconeag Ice Caves

The hike to the Debsconeag Ice Caves passes through a mature evergreen forest full of huge boulders. The hike would be worth doing even without the ice caves at its end. The trail splits at the end, leading to a rocky overlook of First Debsconeag Lake, the ice caves, and a steep descent to the lakeshore. Be sure to bring a flashlight to explore the boulders for caves; many have ice in them year-round.

Start: Ice Caves parking area at the end of the Hurd Pond Road
Elevation gain: 555 feet
Distance: 2.5 miles out and back
Hiking time: 2–3 hours
Difficulty: Easy
Season: Best June–Sept
Trail surface: Woodland path
Land status: Debsconeag Lakes Wilderness
Nearest town: Millinocket
Other users: None
Water availability: Hurd Brook at the trailhead

Canine compatibility: Dogs not allowed in the Debsconeag Lakes Wilderness
Fees and permits: No fees or permits required
Maps: *DeLorme: Maine Atlas & Gazetteer:* Map 50; USGS Abol Pond
Trail contact: The Nature Conservancy; nature.org/maine
Amenities available: Outhouse near parking area
Maximum grade: 57% for short distance below leaning rock to the lakeshore
Cell service: None

Finding the trailhead: From exit 244 on I-95, drive west on ME 157 toward Millinocket and Baxter State Park. Drive 11.8 miles into Millinocket, where ME 157 ends at a T intersection. Turn right onto Katahdin Avenue, toward Baxter State Park. Drive 8.8 miles to where the road passes between Millinocket and Ambajejus Lakes; there is a store and several lodges at this busy spot. Continue driving 1.3 miles to the left turn for Golden Road; there are several signs for commercial camps and the Allagash at the turn. Cut across to Golden Road and turn right, heading north. Drive 9 miles on the Golden Road to Abol Bridge. Just across the bridge, turn left onto a wide, unmarked gravel road and continue 0.1 mile to a Nature Conservancy information kiosk. Drive 3.9 miles to where the road is gated at Hurd Pond Brook. There is a marked parking area on the right. Begin the hike by crossing the bridge over the stream. Trailhead GPS: N45° 47.484' / W68° 58.703'

The Hike

The Debsconeag Lakes are within The Nature Conservancy's Debsconeag Lakes Wilderness. The eight lakes and ponds are all entirely undeveloped, except for a commercial camp on Fourth Lake. Debsconeag means "carrying place" in the Penobscot language. The first four lakes are connected by short carries, or canoe portages, alongside streams. The lakes are also within carrying distance of Nahmakanta Lake, part of a water highway that connects Maine to the St. Lawrence River.

First Debsconeag Lake is connected to the Debsconeag Deadwater on the West Branch Penobscot River by a wide, shallow thoroughfare. The long, narrow lake is

The rock garden

140 feet deep at its center. The north shore of the lake is a low ridge of loose boulders covered with a thin veneer of soil and moss. Where large gaps in the boulders exist, there are caves that can hold ice all summer. The caves are not solutional caves where water has dissolved limestone—such as Mammoth Cave or Carlsbad Caverns—but simply gaps between the ill-fitting boulders. There are numerous ice caves in Maine, but the Debsconeag Ice Caves are the easiest to hike to and among the largest.

The hike begins where Hurd Pond Road is gated at a bridge over Hurd Pond Stream. The trail winds through second growth before entering a forest of mature hemlocks and pines. There is very little growing beneath the tall trees, but the forest floor is littered with moss and fern-covered boulders. Some of the boulders are as big as houses. These boulders are tightly nestled into the forest floor, with few gaps around their edges; but what gaps do exist hint at what awaits you at the end of the trail. The trail wanders from boulder to boulder, gently climbing to the crest of the hill above First Debsconeag Lake. The easy walk would be worth doing even without the ice caves to visit.

Just before the trail begins to descend to the lake, a side trail heads west to the top of a rocky promontory. You can stand on the exposed bedrock alongside two huge boulders and look out across First Debsconeag Lake. You can see Debsconeag

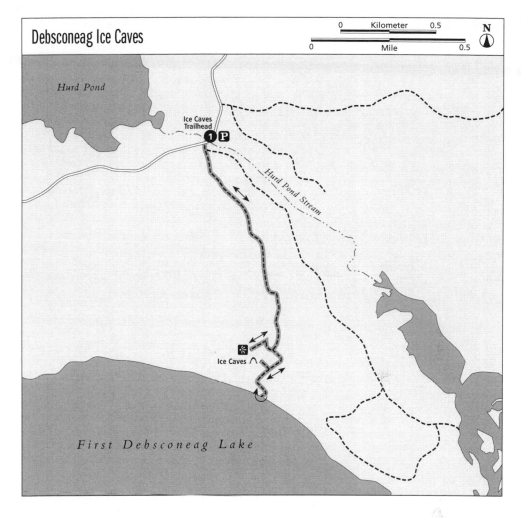

Hurd Pond

Ice Caves
Trailhead

1 **P**

Hurd Pond Stream

Ice Caves

First Debsconeag Lake

0   Kilometer   0.5

0   Mile   0.5

N

Deadwater to the east and hear Debsconeag Falls on the West Branch. To the west, hidden by the seemingly endless forest, is Second Debsconeag Lake. Directly below this vantage point lies a jumble of boulders, dropping away to the lakeshore. The ice caves are hidden in these boulders.

The trail drops down from the overlook trail to another side trail that leads to the ice caves. The ice caves trail ends at a huge boulder that is the roof of the largest ice cave. Iron rungs have been driven into the rock, allowing you to climb down into the cave. Bring a flashlight so you can explore the cave's nooks and crannies. The air in the cave is cool, even on hot days; ice remains on the floor year-round. There are many smaller caves in this boulder field. As you explore the uneven terrain, be careful not to damage the fragile mosses and other ground cover.

The trail continues down to the lake from the ice caves side trail. Along the way it passes a number of smaller caves and a boulder that overhangs a sandy area that looks

First Debsconeag Lake from the overlook

like it could have been used as a camping spot for thousands of years. For years, the only easy way to visit the ice caves was to paddle up First Debsconeag Lake to where the trail ends on the shore and hike uphill to the caves. Several signs hang on trees at the end of the trail, pointing canoeists to the caves. Between the end of the trail and the east end of the pond, there are many more caves in the woods, beneath towering hemlocks and pines, but no trail to them. Looking back uphill, the way you came, it's hard to believe that the forest before you overlays so much empty space.

Miles and Directions

0.0   Start by crossing the bridge over Hurd Pond Brook behind the red gate.

100 feet   Bear left off the woods road onto a marked hiking trail.

0.8   The trail wanders through the woods, among pines and large boulders to a junction. Turn right to hike to the overlook.

0.9   Arrive at the overlook. The trail ends atop a cliff with several large boulders sitting on top of it. You have views of First Debsconeag Lake; to the east you can see Debsconeag Deadwater on the Penobscot River and hear Debsconeag Falls. Return to the trail junction and turn right.

1.1   The trail forks again. Turn right to go to the ice caves.

1.2   The trail ends at the Debsconeag Ice Caves. There is a set of iron rungs down into the largest ice cave. After exploring the jumbled boulders for ice caves, return to the trail junction and turn right to descend to First Debsconeag Lake.

1.4   The trail descends past large boulders to First Debsconeag Lake. To complete the hike, return the way you came.

2.5   Arrive back at the trailhead.

2 Horserace Pond

The hike visits several ponds, including the gorgeous Horserace Pond. Between the ponds is a high ridge with many open ledges. You have views south and northeast to nearby Katahdin. This hike in the northwest corner of the 100 Mile Wilderness is a beautiful cap on the region.

Start: Horserace Pond Trailhead
Elevation gain: 1,968 feet
Distance: 9.3-mile lollipop
Hiking time: 5–6 hours
Difficulty: Strenuous
Season: June–Oct
Trail surface: Woodland path
Land status: Debsconeag Lakes Wilderness
Nearest town: Millinocket
Other users: None
Water availability: Horserace Brook and Horserace Pond

Canine compatibility: Dogs not allowed in Debsconeag Lakes Wilderness
Fees and permits: No fees or permits required
Maps: *DeLorme: Maine Atlas & Gazetteer:* Map 50; USGS Rainbow Lake East
Trail contact: The Nature Conservancy; nature.org/maine
Amenities available: Privy near trailhead and at campsite on Horserace Pond
Maximum grade: 15% descent for 0.4 mile from ridge to Horserace Pond; 15% climb for 0.3 mile on Blue Trail to ridgetop
Cell service: None

Finding the trailhead: From exit 244 on I-95, drive west on ME 157 toward Millinocket and Baxter State Park. Drive 11.8 miles into Millinocket, where ME 157 ends at a T intersection. Turn right onto Katahdin Avenue toward Baxter State Park. Drive 8.8 miles to where the road passes between Millinocket and Ambajejus Lakes; there is a store and several lodges at this busy spot. Continue driving 1.3 miles to the left turn for Golden Road; there are several signs for commercial camps and the Allagash at the turn. Cut across to Golden Road and turn right, heading north. Drive 9 miles on Golden Road to Abol Bridge. Continue on Golden Road another 5.2 miles. Turn left onto the access road at the sign for the Rainbow Loop Trail and Horserace Pond. Drive 0.2 mile to the end of the road. The trailhead is at the bridge across Horserace Brook Trailhead GPS: N45° 50.887' / W69° 04.194'

The Hike

The trail crosses Horserace Brook on a stout bridge near where the brook flows into Nesowadnehunk Deadwater on the West Branch. You wander though low, rocky forest, following an old roadbed some of the time. You even pass through an old roadcut. When you reach a junction, turn left onto the Blue Trail.

Climb steadily up several cliffy ledges in the forest. Reach another junction on the crest of the ridge; go straight, staying on the Blue Trail. Descend steadily to Clifford Pond. Don't bushwhack to the pond the first chance you get; a short side trail leads to the pond just ahead. Across the pond, irregular masses of bedrock break up the forest that hugs the shore.

Small pond nestled on the ridge

The trail continues, descending very gently to Woodman Pond. The trail along the pond is overgrown with ferns and huckleberry bushes but easy to follow. An unmarked side trail leads down to the shore. Across the pond, the ridge with exposed ledges crossed by the Rainbow Loop Trail is visible.

From Woodman Pond, the trail descends very gently to a giant boulder in the woods, then descends steadily. The trail ends at a shallow cove on Rainbow Lake. From here Rainbow Lake looks quite large—and you can see less than half of it. This cove is a good place to see wildlife. From here, retrace your steps to the junction atop the ridge and turn left onto the orange-blazed Rainbow Loop Trail.

The trail descends gently into a saddle, then climbs to the first overlook. You have a view south of Clifford Pond with mountains in the background. The trail roller-coasters along ledges climbing to a small marshy pond. The trail climbs to the left above the pond before reaching another more expansive overlook. From here you can see most of Rainbow Lake, with the hump of Rainbow Mountain behind it. Off to the right you can see Chesuncook Lake.

Katadhin from the ledges

The trail wanders over more ledges and reaches a pretty pond tucked against the ridge. The trail loops around the end of the pond to climb the ridge. Up on the ridge, you get your first view of Katahdin from a large hump of bedrock the trail climbs using a crack. From there it's a short distance to the most open ledge yet. You have expansive views south and west. To the east and northeast, views of Katahdin and Mount O-J-I are only partially blocked by trees.

After soaking in the view, follow the trail back into the woods and descend steadily. Through a mossy spruce forest littered with ledges and large boulders, you drop to Horserace Pond. The trail reaches the shore near its east end. The shoreline is composed of boulders and bedrock slabs that tilt into the deep water. Across the pond, the forest rises so steeply that swaths of it are bare rock. It's a spectacular swimming hole.

Near the east end of the pond, amid giant boulders, are two campsites and a privy. At the outlet you turn right onto the Horserace Pond Trail. Take this trail back to the trailhead, descending very gradually beside a babbling Horserace Brook.

Horserace Pond

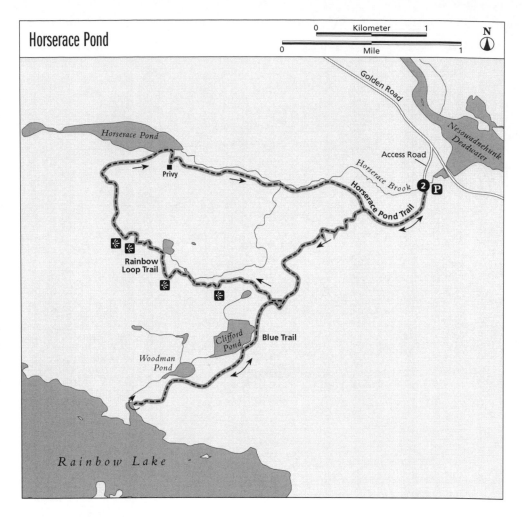

Miles and Directions

0.0 Start by crossing Horserace Brook on the bridge.

0.6 Turn left onto the Blue Trail.

1.6 Climb through bouldery forest and up several ledges to the junction with the orange-blazed Rainbow Loop Trail. Pass this trail.

2.1 Descend steadily to a side trail that leads 100 feet to the shore of Clifford Pond.

2.6 Pass near Woodman Pond. A rough unmarked trail leads through dense ferns and shrubs to the shore.

3.0 Descend gently then steeply once you pass a large erratic to the shore of Rainbow Lake. To continue the hike, retrace your steps to the junction with the Rainbow Loop Trail.

4.4 Arrive back at the junction. Turn left onto the Rainbow Loop Trail.

5.0 Descend gently, then climb to a ledge with a fine view of Clifford Pond.

Horserace Pond

5.3 Descend off the ledge and climb to a small pond nestled against cliffs.

5.5 Climb away from the pond to open ledges.

5.6 Descend gently to a larger pond.

5.9 Climb away from the pond to a large, rounded ledge with a view of Katahdin.

6.1 Descend slightly, then climb to a large open ledge at the high point of the hike. From this ledge you have open views south and west, with partial views northeast to Katahdin and Mount O-J-I.

7.1 Descend steadily through a bouldery forest, then more gently to the shore of Horserace Pond.

7.3 Wind among the large boulders along the shore of the pond to the outlet stream.

8.4 Follow Horserace Brook away from the pond, eventually turning away from the brook.

8.7 Pass the Blue Trail.

9.3 Arrive back at the trailhead.

3 Lower Bean Pond and Rainbow Deadwaters

This remote hike visits the two Rainbow Deadwaters: Murphy Pond and Lower Bean Pond. The walking is all easy through varied woods, with lots of wildflowers and the possibility of wildlife.

Start: Parking area at the end of Wadleigh Pond Road

Elevation gain: 1,206 feet

Distance: 7.8 miles out and back

Hiking time: About 4 hours

Difficulty: Moderate because of distance

Season: June–Nov

Trail surface: Abandoned woods roads and woodland trails

Land status: Debsconeag Lakes Wilderness

Nearest town: Milo

Other users: Hunters and anglers in season

Water availability: Filterable water in several streams and ponds

Canine compatibility: Dogs not allowed in the Debsconeag Lakes Wilderness

Fees and permits: Access fee paid at Jo-Mary gatehouse

Maps: *DeLorme: Maine Atlas & Gazetteer:* Map 50; USGS Rainbow Lake West

Trail contact: The Nature Conservancy's Debsconeag Lakes Wilderness Area; nature.org/en-us/get-involved/how-to-help/places-we-protect/debsconeag-lakes-wilderness-area/

Amenities available: None

Maximum grade: 12% descent to Bean Brook for 0.4 mile

Cell service: None

Finding the trailhead: Drive north on ME 11 out of Brownville for 15.7 miles from the bridge over the Pleasant River. Turn left onto Jo-Mary Road (at the sign for Jo-Mary Campground) and drive 0.1 mile. Stop and pay the entrance fee. Continue on Jo-Mary Road for another 6 miles. Turn right, staying on Jo-Mary Road for 16.2 miles. Pass the parking areas for the Turtle Ridge and Tumbledown Dick Trailheads and continue another 3.9 miles. Turn right at the intersection onto Wadleigh Pond Road. Continue 5.2 miles, passing Nahmakanta Stream Road, two campsites, and Pollywog Pond Road. You will come to a small parking area on the left and then cross the Appalachian Trail. Continue for another 2 miles. You will pass another parking area on the right, then the AT joins the road. Cross Pollywog Stream; across the bridge, go straight and continue 1.2 miles. The road reaches a wide grassy area; park here. The road continues but is much narrower. Begin the hike by walking up the continuation of the road. Trailhead GPS: N45° 47.234' / W69° 10.903'

The Hike

First you hike up the continuation of the road to Murphy Pond, passing a junction along the way. This irregularly shaped pond is surrounded by dense spruce and swampy ground. It feels very wild and looks like good moose habitat, especially across the pond near its outlet. After scanning the pond and its shoreline for moose and ducks, head back to the junction and turn right onto the green-blazed trail.

The trail wanders through the woods and drops gently to a pond. On the right, an unmarked trail leads 750 feet to the Rainbow Stream Lean-to on the AT. The

Outlet of Upper Rainbow Deadwater

unnamed pond has a wide marshy fringe. An obvious but unmarked side trail leads out though this verge to a rocky spot on the pond's shore.

Past the pond, the trail reaches a junction. To the left, Bean Pond is down the blue-blazed trail; to the right are the Rainbow Deadwaters on the green-blazed trail. Turn right and, in a short distance, turn right again onto a red-blazed trail. This trail leads to the south shore of the lower deadwater. You can bushwhack to the right around the shore to the outlet, where there's a pretty waterfall.

Back on the green-blazed trail, you head toward the upper (and much larger) deadwater. You can see the stream through the woods to your right. An unmarked trail drops down to the stream, where it passes through a meadow. The trail turns right off the roadbed that has been the green-blazed trail and descends to the south shore of the upper deadwater. At the outlet you have a nice view of the deadwater nestled into low hills.

Retrace your steps to the blue-blazed trail and turn right. The trail wanders through the woods then descends gently down a hillside of large bedrock slabs covered in moss and lichen. The trail reaches Bean Brook and turns right to follow the brook upstream. The stream is slow and marshy, so the trail stays back away from it in the woods. Again, this is good moose habitat.

The trail ends at the south shore of Lower Bean Pond. The best view is from rocks at the mouth of the outlet. In front of you is the oval pond crowded in by forest;

Waterfall at the outlet of the lower Rainbow Deadwater

behind you, the marshy brook turns a bend and disappears into the trees. Sitting on a rock here eating lunch, you're a long way from anywhere.

Miles and Directions

0.0   Start by hiking up the continuation of the road.

0.6   Arrive at a blazed intersection. Bear right onto the blue-blazed trail.

0.9   Arrive at Murphy Pond. To continue the hike, retrace your steps to the intersection.

1.2   Arrive back at the intersection. Turn right onto the green-blazed trail.

1.4   Descend to a small pond, visible to the left through the trees.

1.6   Pass an unmarked trail on the right that leads 750 feet to the Rainbow Stream Lean-to on the AT.

1.7   An unmarked but obvious trail on the left leads 100 feet to the shore of the pond.

1.8   Reach a junction with another blue-blazed trail. Bear right, staying on the green-blazed trail.

1.9   As you pass the junction, you can hear Rainbow Stream. Reach another junction; turn right onto the red-blazed trail.

2.0   Reach the south shore of the lower Rainbow Deadwater.

2.1   Bushwhack along the shore toward the sound of Rainbow Stream. When you reach the stream, bushwhack downstream to a small slide and waterfall. To continue your hike, retrace your steps to the green-blazed trail.

2.3   Arrive back at the green-blazed trail. Turn right.

2.4   An unmarked but obvious trail leads 100 feet to the shore of the lower deadwater near its north end.

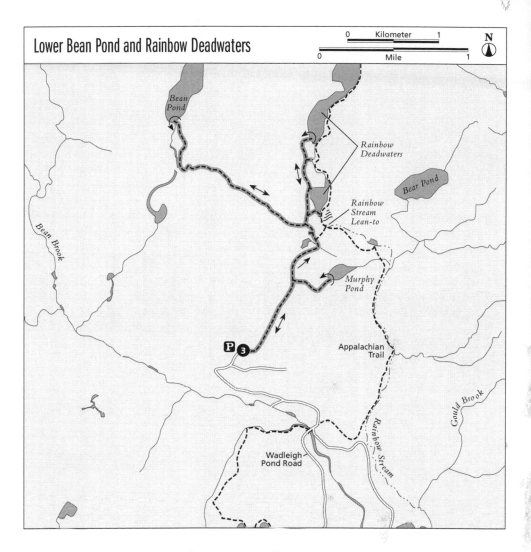

0   Kilometer   1

N

0   Mile   1

Bean Pond

Rainbow Deadwaters

Bear Pond

Rainbow Stream Lean-to

Bean Brook

Murphy Pond

P 3

Appalachian Trail

Gould Brook

Rainbow Stream

Wadleigh Pond Road

2.8 The trail follows Rainbow Stream upstream. The trail turns right.

2.9 Reach the south shore of the upper Rainbow Deadwater. To continue your hike, follow the green-blazed trail back to the intersection with the blue-blazed trail.

3.7 Turn right onto the blue-blazed trail.

4.7 The trail climbs gently, with high, moss-covered cliffs on the left. Reach a saddle and descend through a ravine with low cliffs on both sides. Through the ravine, the trail descends more steeply to Bean Brook.

5.1 The trail follows Bean Brook to Bean Pond. To complete the hike, retrace your steps to the green-blazed trail.

6.5 Arrive back at the green-blazed trail; bear right.

7.2 Arrive back at the first intersection. Bear right, staying on the green-blazed trail.

7.8 Arrive back at the trailhead.

4 Rainbow Stream

Rainbow Stream flows out of Rainbow Lake and through a series of deadwaters, then crashes down a long hillside to Nahmakanta Lake. This hike follows the stream past the numerous waterfalls and slides in that descent.

Start: Bridge over Pollywog Stream on Wadleigh Pond Road
Elevation gain: 592 feet
Distance: 4.8 miles out and back
Hiking time: About 3 hours
Difficulty: Easy
Season: June–Oct
Trail surface: Woodland path
Land status: Appalachian Trail
Nearest town: Brownville
Other users: None
Water availability: Rainbow Stream
Canine compatibility: Dogs must be under control at all times.

Fees and permits: Access fee paid at the Jo-Mary gatehouse
Maps: *DeLorme: Maine Atlas & Gazetteer:* Map 50; USGS Rainbow Lake West
Trail contact: Nahmakanta Public Reserved Land; (207) 941-4412; maine.gov/nahmakanta
  KI Jo-Mary Forest; (207) 435-6213; northmainewoods.org
Amenities available: None
Maximum grade: Less than 3% average for climb beside the stream
Cell service: None

Finding the trailhead: Drive north on ME 11 out of Brownville for 15.7 miles from the bridge over the Pleasant River. Turn left onto Jo-Mary Road (at the sign for Jo-Mary Campground) and drive 0.1 mile. Stop and pay the entrance fee. Continue on Jo-Mary Road for another 6 miles. Turn right, staying on Jo-Mary Road for 16.2 miles. Pass the parking areas for the Turtle Ridge and Tumbledown Dick Trailheads. Continue another 3.9 miles and turn right at the intersection onto Wadleigh Pond Road. Drive 5.2 miles, passing Nahmakanta Stream RMAP: s [plural]oad, two campsites, and Pollywog Pond Road. You will come to a small parking area on the left and then cross the Appalachian Trail. Continue driving for another 2 miles; the marked parking area is on the right. Start the hike 0.1 mile farther down the road, at the bridge over Pollywog Stream. Trailhead GPS: N45° 46.764' / W69° 10.344'

The Hike

Follow the AT across Pollywog Stream, along the road for a short distance then into the woods. You cross uneven ground between Pollywog Stream and Rainbow Stream. The trail follows beside Rainbow Stream past numerous waterfalls and slides. Lower down, the drops tend to be slides and bedrock joint sluices. These are quite picturesque and easy to access from the trail. Higher up, the falls tend to be drops and plunges—nothing too high, but fine all the same. At one spot about a mile into the hike, Rainbow Stream and a side stream each drop 10 feet into the same pool.

Waterfall on Rainbow Stream

Waterfall on Rainbow Stream

Above this double waterfall are several more drops before you reach a flooded meadow. The stream snakes though tall grasses and boulders. The trail then leaves the stream, looping through the woods to the Rainbow Stream Lean-to, which sits in a stand of giant pines beside the stream. Upstream, you can see the stream emerging around a bend beside irregular cliffs.

If you're feeling ambitious, you can cross the stream and continue northbound on the AT. It's a short distance to the first deadwater. Or you can head back downstream and re-enjoy all the waterfalls.

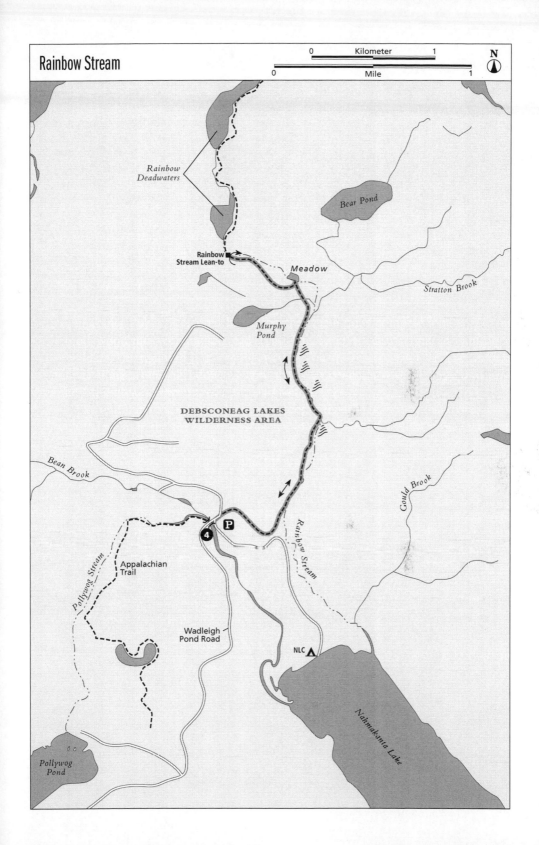

Double waterfall on Rainbow Stream

Miles and Directions

0.0 Start from the bridge over Pollywog Stream on Wadleigh Pond Road. Walk farther up the road, passing the road on the right that leads to Nahmakanta Lake Camps. In 100 feet, turn right off the road onto the Appalachian Trail at the small cairn.

0.5 Reach Rainbow Stream.

1.1 The trail follows alongside the stream past several small waterfalls and slides. Reach a double fall where Rainbow Stream and a side stream both drop into a pool.

1.6 Pass several more waterfalls.

2.0 Reach a wet meadow the stream flows through.

2.4 Reach the Rainbow Stream Lean-to. The AT crosses Rainbow Stream and passes through a small gorge. To complete the hike retrace your steps to the trailhead.

4.8 Arrive back at the trailhead.

5 Debsconeag Backcountry, West Loop

This hike passes the upper Debsconeag Ponds and two pretty beaver ponds. You cross bare ledges and hike beneath cliffs. Along the shore of Nahmakanta Lake, you have fine views of Nesuntabunt Mountain and access to a sandy beach.

Start: Debsconeag Backcountry Trailhead West
Elevation gain: 1,531 feet
Distance: 8.9-mile lollipop
Hiking time: 5–6 hours
Difficulty: Moderate; easy but long hike
Season: June–Oct
Trail surface: Woodland path
Land status: Nahmakanta Public Reserved Land
Nearest town: Brownville
Other users: Hunters in season
Water availability: Spring at mile 5.6
Canine compatibility: Dogs must be under control at all times.

Fees and permits: Access fee paid at the Jo-Mary gatehouse
Maps: *DeLorme: Maine Atlas & Gazetteer:* Map 50; USGS Rainbow Lake West and Rainbow Lake East
Trail contact: Nahmakanta Public Reserved Land; (207) 941-4412; maine.gov/nahmakanta KI Jo-Mary Forest; (207) 435-6213; northmainewoods.org
Amenities available: None
Maximum grade: 10% grade on climb from stream ford to first overlook
Cell service: None

Finding the trailhead: Drive north on ME 11 out of Brownville for 15.7 miles from the bridge over the Pleasant River. Turn left onto Jo-Mary Road (at the sign for Jo-Mary Campground) and drive 0.1 mile. Stop and pay the entrance fee. Continue on Jo-Mary Road for another 6 miles. Turn right, staying on Jo-Mary Road for 16.2 miles. Pass the parking areas for the Turtle Ridge and Tumbledown Dick Trailheads. Continue another 3.9 miles and turn right at the intersection onto Wadleigh Pond Road. Drive 5.2 miles, passing Nahmakanta Stream Road, two campsites, and Pollywog Pond Road. You will come to a small parking area on the left and then cross the Appalachian Trail. Continue for another 2 miles. Pass a parking area on the right and cross Pollywog Stream. Turn right toward NLC and drive 0.5 mile. The parking lot is on the right; the trailhead is across the road. Trailhead GPS: N45° 46.684' / W69° 09.903'

The Hike

Plan your trip knowing that the ford of Rainbow Stream can be dangerous when the water's high. In summer, the water is usually shin deep and refreshing. Across the stream, the trail climbs gently up a rocky hillside to ledges with a nice view of Nahmakanta Lake. From the ledges, descend gently, again through rocks, to a bridge over Gould Brook. Turn left (the trail to the right will be your return route).

The trail climbs gently beside Gould Brook through hardwoods, then turns east. You pass two side trails that head north to Gould Pond used mostly by anglers. The trail continues to climb gently, skirting the north side of a hill. You pass a long line of cliffs then descend gently to a beaver pond. The trail skirts a beaver pond then Eighth

Nahmakanta Lake, with Nesuntabunt Mountain on the far shore

Debsconeag Pond and another beaver pond. Each pond is unique and pretty in its own way. This is a good area to see moose.

The trail crosses the stream that connects these ponds to Seventh Debsconeag Pond and climbs to ledges. These ledges run for nearly a mile. Open areas with partial views are connected by wooded section and small climbs. Blueberries and lichen are everywhere. Random boulders sit on the ledges among widely spaced spruce and birch trees.

Turn right at a junction (the sign faces the other way and is unhelpful). Descend steadily down a series of ledges with fine views south. The trail drops into the woods above Seventh Debsconeag Pond. As you hike around the pond, take time to climb atop the large boulder just off the trail. You'll have a great view of the pond, a good place to see wildlife. The trail continues around the pond and crosses the outlet on a ledge.

Across the ledge, the trail works through some rocks and wanders through the woods to Sixth Debsconeag Pond. An obvious but unmarked side trail leads 200 feet to a ledge on the shore of the pond. Just past this side trail, turn right onto an unmarked trail.

Descend gently toward Nahmakanta Lake. The trail passes through a wide, low gorge with a reliable spring. As you reach the lake, the trail turns right and follows the shoreline. You get off-and-on views across the lake of Nesuntabunt Mountain. Watch for the sand beach a little more than 0.5 mile past where you first reached the lakeshore.

The trail follows the shoreline to the northeast end, turning away where the end of the lake gets swampy. This is where Gould Brook and Rainbow Stream flow into the lake. Climb gently beside Gould Brook to the intersection with the bridge over the brook to close the loop. Now you just have the enjoyable and rocky hike back down the lollipop's stick to the trailhead.

Cliffs along the trail

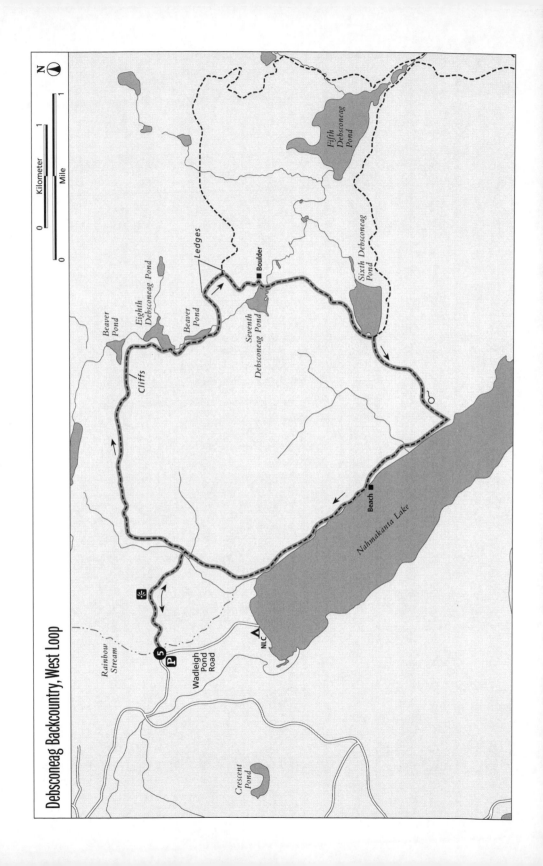

Debsconeag Backcountry, West Loop

Beaver flowage

Miles and Directions

0.0 Start at the Debsconeag Backcountry west trailhead. In 200 feet, ford Rainbow Stream. (**Note:** This crossing can be hazardous during high water.)

0.1 Begin climbing away from Rainbow Stream.

0.5 Reach a ledge with a fine view of Nahmakanta Lake and Nesuntabunt Mountain.

0.9 Cross Gould Brook and turn left.

2.3 Pass two trails to Gould Pond; hike beside high cliffs.

2.4 Descend to a beaver flowage.

2.6 Reach Eighth Debsconeag Pond.

3.0 Pass a second beaver flowage.

3.2 Cross an outlet stream.

3.3 Climb to ledges.

3.4 On ledges, reach an intersection. Turn right.

4.0 Descend ledges with views to Seventh Debsconeag Pond.

4.1 Cross an outlet stream.

4.9 Pass an unmarked trail on the left that leads 200 feet to Sixth Debsconeag Pond.

5.0 Turn right at a junction.

5.6 Descend through a gorge with a spring.

5.8 Reach the shore of Nahmakanta Lake.

6.5 Hike along the shore of the lake with views. Pass a small sand beach.

7.5 As you approach the head of the lake, the trail bends right and begins to climb.

8.0 Climb gently to the bridge over Gould Brook. Turn left and cross the bridge.

8.9 Arrive back at the trailhead.

6 Debsconeag Backcountry, East Loop

This hike through remote woodlands is difficult only because of its length. The hike visits four of the Debsconeag Lakes and Ponds. Each is very different, but all offer excellent wildlife viewing opportunities. The surrounding woods, much of it towering mature trees, also offers good chances to see wildlife, especially moose. From the ledges above Seventh Debsconeag Pond, you get fine views to the west, north, and south. The trail is lightly maintained but fairly easy to follow because of good blazing.

Start: Parking area on the north side of Nahmakanta Stream Road, 1 mile from the bridge over Nahmakanta Stream

Distance: 9.2-mile loop

Hiking time: 5–7 hours

Difficulty: Moderate

Season: Best June–Oct

Trail surface: Woodland path

Land status: Nahmakanta Public Reserved Land

Nearest town: Brownville

Other users: Hunting permitted on Maine Public Reserved Lands; anglers use the trails to access the ponds.

Water availability: Trail crosses 3 streams and passes 5 ponds.

Canine compatibility: Dogs must be under control at all times.

Fees and permits: Access fee paid at the Jo-Mary gatehouse

Maps: *DeLorme: Maine Atlas & Gazetteer:* Map 50; USGS Nahmakanta Stream and Rainbow Lake East

Trail contact: Nahmakanta Public Reserved Land; (207) 827-1818; maine.gov/nahmakanta

Amenities available: None

Maximum grade: 11.4% descent from overlook to Stink Pond and down beside outlet stream for 0.9 mile

Cell service: None

Finding the trailhead: From the bridge over the Pleasant River in Brownville, drive north on ME 11 for 15.6 miles. Turn left onto Jo-Mary Road; there is a large sign for Jo-Mary Campground at the intersection. Drive 0.1 mile to the gate; stop and pay fee. Continue 6 miles to a fork in the road; turn right, staying on Jo-Mary Road. Drive 9.9 miles, where you will pass the trailhead parking for Turtle Ridge and Tumbledown Dick Falls. Continue 4 miles to an intersection; turn right onto Wadleigh Pond Road. Drive 0.9 mile to Nahmakanta Stream Road; turn right and continue 1 mile. The road bears right at a fork. Drive another 2 miles, passing the side road to the boat launch at the foot of Nahmakanta Lake. At 0.1 mile beyond the side road, Nahmakanta Stream Road crosses the Appalachian Trail and then Nahmakanta Stream. Across the stream, the road is much rougher, but still passable by most cars. From the bridge, drive 1 mile to the parking lot, on the left. (*Note:* The road continues down to Fourth Debsconeag Lake; do not drive down the hill to the lake.) Start the hike at the trail sign at the back of the parking area. Trailhead GPS: N45° 44.723' / W69° 05.478'

The Hike

The lower Debsconeag Lakes are within The Nature Conservancy's Debsconeag Lakes Wilderness Area; the upper ponds—which this hike visits—are within the

Trail on the ledges

Nahmakanta Public Reserved Land. Together these units compose a huge tract of remote woodlands with limited road access. This means fewer users and an abundance of wildlife. The trailhead is up the hill, west of Fourth Debsconeag Lake. The first 0.8 mile is along a long-abandoned woods road that connects with the loop trail near where the stream flows out of Fifth Debsconeag Lake.

The trail skirts the edge of the marshy foot of the lake before climbing over a hill with ledges near the top. From the ledges you have a partial view of the lake and, across it, the hills you'll be hiking over later.

The trail drops off the ridge and through the forest toward Sixth Debsconeag Pond. There are many wet areas where you may see moose. This open, mixed forest near several ponds and bogs is good habitat for cows with calves.

For a short stretch, the trail follows an old woods road that seems to lead nowhere at either end, a reminder that all these woods were cut at some point in the past. This section of road must have led from somewhere—likely near where you parked—to somewhere cutting was going on, but now it is just a short section of wide trail, a reminder that wilderness is not a characteristic of the land or forest but a use-pattern.

The trail skirts the south side of Sixth Debsconeag Pond and passes a side trail that leads 100 feet to a campsite on the shore. Shortly after, you pass the west loop trail

Nesuntabunt Mountain from the ledges, with Seventh Debsconeag Pond below

that leads to Nahmakanta Lake. Just past the junction, a side trail leads to a rock shelf on the shore of the pond. It's a good place to relax and watch for ducks and moose. On buggy days, trout regularly rise to the surface. You can hear—but not see—the outlet stream leave the pond's far side to tumble through the woods and several bogs to Fifth Debsconeag Lake.

Beyond Sixth Debsconeag Pond, the trail works around a low hill to Seventh Debsconeag Pond. Here the woods are more open and dry, with fewer hardwoods. The trail crosses the outlet stream where bedrock has formed a natural dam that beavers have supplemented. Downstream is an open area of bog the stream winds through. The pond itself is almost as much a meadow as a pond. If it weren't for the beavers raising the water level, the pond may have already become an open, wet meadow. Just past the stream crossing, there is a large boulder along the shore that you can climb to get a good look at the pond. Watch for beaver and ducks.

The trail circles the pond and climbs a series of increasingly open ledges with views to the west and south. You can see Nesuntabunt Mountain across Nahmakanta Lake and the White Cap Range in the distance. Near the top of the ridge, there is an intersection with a trail that leads to the north end of Nahmakanta Lake. The signs at this intersection are confusing at best. Turn right (east) and enter the woods through a

Debsconeag Falls

glade of ferns, watching for blue blazes. The trail crosses more open ledges with views, then drops into the woods.

The trail then wanders through the woods, descending to two brooks. Past the brooks, you climb a ridge to ledges above Stink Pond, with views east and south. From there the trail loops around to the west and descends to the pond. The trail passes near the pond, but not right to it. When you can see the marshy edge of the pond just to your left, take the small side trail if you want to explore the pond. The marshy rim of Stink Pond is good habitat for plants such as liverwort and other northern bog species. Watch for moose and ducks here as well.

The trail drops away from the pond to where the outlet stream falls down a wide shelf of exposed bedrock. The trail loops out across the rock, which can be challenging and slippery when the water is running high. The trail follows the stream down as it tumbles noisily over boulders and ledges toward Fifth Debsconeag Lake. The trail crosses the stream three times, the last time on a wide boulder the stream crosses in a crack and then drops into a small pool. The trail levels out and passes through a grove of old-growth hemlock. A side trail leads out to Fifth Debsconeag Lake. You can see the open ledges on the hills around the lake. Past the side trail, you hike across an old dam in the woods and then come to the junction along the stream above the waterfall.

Bear left and descend beside the brook through a mossy gorge. You pass a beautiful waterfall, with unmarked access to the top, middle, and bottom of the falls. Below the falls, the trail levels out and then ends at the road to Chewonki's Debsconeag Lake Camps. Turn right and follow the road back to your car, walking along the shore of Fourth Debsconeag Lake much of the way.

Miles and Directions

0.0 Start at the marked trailhead at the back of the parking area.

0.8 The trail follows an old road bed then descends to a side trail that drops down to the brook that flows out of Fifth Debsconeag Lake. Continue past the trail.

1.7 The trail follows along the shore of the lake then climbs a hill to ledges. There used to be a fine view from the ledges, but the trees have grown sufficiently to block much of the view.

2.6 Pass a side trail that leads to a campsite on Sixth Debsconeag Pond.

2.9 Pass an unmarked trail on the left. This is the trail that leads to Nahmakanta Lake.

3.0 Turn right on an unmarked side trail that leads in 200 feet to ledges on the shore of the pond.

3.1 Return to the main trail; turn right.

3.8 The trail wanders through the woods. This section is less used and more overgrown. Descend to and cross Seventh Debsconeag Pond's outlet stream.

3.9 A large boulder just off the trail offers a fine view of the pond.

4.3 Climb increasingly open ledges with nice views to a junction; turn right.

4.5 Cross more ledges, reaching one with a fine open view.

5.0 Descend off the ledges to a small brook.

5.1 Descend further and cross a larger brook.

6.0 Climb gently but without stopping to ledges with a fine view of Stink Pond and the lakes and mountains beyond.

6.3 Loop through the woods to a second ledge. Descend the ledge.

6.8 Reach Stink Pond. An unmarked trail leads 50 feet to the shore.

6.9 Descend to open ledges that Stink Pond's outlet flows down. The trail is only on the ledges for 50 feet before turning back into the woods.

7.2 Descend beside the stream, crossing it three times.

7.5 Bear right onto an unmarked side trail.

7.6 Reach the shore of Fifth Debsconeag Lake. Retrace your steps to the main trail.

7.7 Turn right, back onto the main trail.

8.0 Pass through a bouldery area, cross an old dam, and arrive at the outlet stream. A marked trail descends to and crosses the brook. It then climbs 0.1 mile to where you were at mile 0.8. Bear left and descend beside the brook.

8.1 Reach the top of Debsconeag Brook Falls.

8.2 Descend beside the waterfall. There are two places you can step off-trail and get nice views of the mossy, joint-slide waterfall.

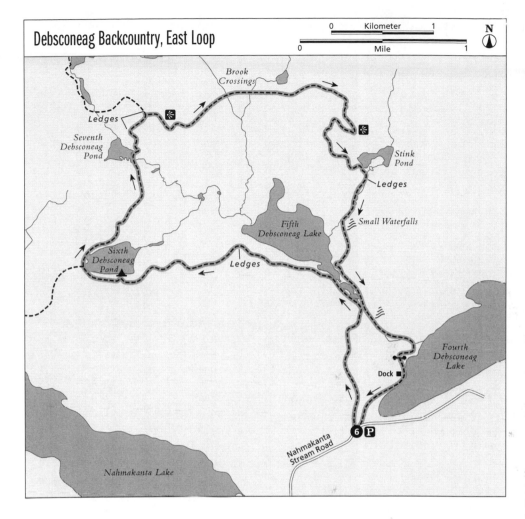

8.4 Past the falls, the trail levels out and ends at a woods road. Turn right. (**Option:** Turn left and follow the road 0.1 mile to Debsconeag Lakes Camps (owned by Chewonki). The historic camps sit on a beautiful peninsula.

8.6 Pass under a gate and bear left, staying on the woods road.

8.8 Pass a dock on the lake.

9.2 Climb away from the lake and arrive back at the trailhead.

7 Nesuntabunt Mountain from the North

Nesuntabunt Mountain rises in a wilderness of irregular hills and ponds. This short hike leads through an old-growth forest of white pine and red spruce to a spectacular view of Katahdin. The trailhead may be 25 miles from the nearest paved road, but it's worth the trip.

Start: Appalachian Trail crossing on Wadleigh Pond Road
Distance: 2.4 miles out and back
Elevation gain: 647 feet
Hiking time: 1–2 hours
Difficulty: Moderate
Season: May–Oct
Trail surface: Woodland path
Land status: Appalachian Trail within Nahmakanta Public Reserved Land
Nearest town: Brownville
Other users: Hunting allowed within Maine Reserved Lands
Water availability: None

Canine compatibility: Dogs must be under control at all times.
Fees and permits: Access fee paid at the Jo-Mary gatehouse
Maps: *DeLorme: Maine Atlas & Gazetteer:* Maps 50 and 42; USGS Wadleigh Mountain
Trail contact: Nahmakanta Public Reserved Land; (207) 941-4412; maine.gov/nahmakanta
KI Jo-Mary Forest; (207) 435-6213; northmainewoods.org
Amenities available: None
Maximum grade: 8% on climb from first overlook to top of cliffs for 0.4 mile
Cell service: None

Finding the trailhead: From the bridge over the Pleasant River in Brownville on ME 11, drive north 15.7 miles. Turn left onto Jo-Mary Road at the Jo-Mary Campground sign. The gate where you pay the fee is 0.1 mile from ME 11. From the gate, drive 5.9 miles to a fork in the road. Bear right, staying on Jo-Mary Road. At 11.4 miles from the gate, you cross a stream and the Appalachian Trail. At 15.8 miles from the gate, you pass the Turtle Ridge Trail. At 19.7 miles from the gate, you come to a T intersection; turn right onto Wadleigh Pond Road. At 20.6 miles from the gate, the road bends left and a smaller road goes straight; bear left, staying on Wadleigh Pond Road. At 21.6 miles from the first gate, pass Nahmakanta Stream Road on the right. At 24.9 miles from the gate, just past the Pollywog Pond Road, there will be a small, unmarked parking area on the left. Turn in here and park. The AT is 50 feet farther down the road. The hike follows the southbound AT on the east side of the road, across from the parking area. Trailhead GPS: N45° 45.809' / W69° 10.540'

The Hike

Nesuntabunt Mountain is a small, rocky summit among rolling hills and scattered ponds. Its eastern face, much of it exposed cliffs, drops to Nahmakanta Lake. It is 25 miles from the nearest paved road in the heart of the Nahmakanta Public Reserved Land, which is surrounded by protected lands owned by The Nature Conservancy, the Appalachian Mountain Club, and others. The Appalachian Trail passes over the north summit of the mountain on its way to Katahdin, 21 trail miles to the north.

Snow-covered Katahdin from Nesuntabunt Mountain

The hike follows the southbound AT from Wadleigh Pond Road through a mixed forest dominated by maple and beech. Be on the lookout for spring wildflowers, especially blood trillium and trout lilies, blooming before the hardwoods leaf out and cast the forest floor into shade for the summer. As the trail gently climbs, the hillside becomes rockier and more of the trees, spruce and fir. Across a seasonal stream that cuts a wide swath through the woods, the trail comes to a ledge of granite overlooking Nahmakanta Lake. Across the lake, some 13 miles away, Katahdin looms. In some years its crown remains snow-covered as late as July. Through the summer the bare granite mountain creates its own weather and is often capped by a cloud even on bright sunny days. As you contemplate the view, look for the white specks of common terns flying low over Nahmakanta Lake. These gull-like birds nest on rocks sticking out of the lakes and ponds in the area. They congregate in loud colonies, adults flying in and out while their nestlings squawk for food.

The AT leaves the overlook, turning toward Nesuntabunt's summit across a wide, wooded ledge between the cliffs down to the lake and cliff up to the mountain's summit. The granite cliffs are giant stairs from the lake to the summit. The trail climbs one step and then slabs around to the north side of the mountain through an open forest of old-growth white pine and red spruce. Because of the thin soil on this steep

Halfway up the cliffs

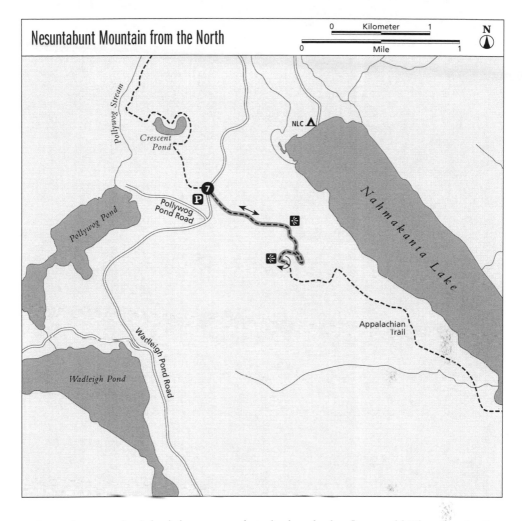

0   Kilometer   1

0   Mile   1

N

slope, the trees don't look large enough to be hundreds of years old. They stand tall and straight, marching up the increasingly steep slope and around the west side of the mountain with little growing beneath them.

The trail climbs straight up through the forest to the summit. The AT turns west and descends the mountain to the shore of Nahmakanta Lake. The hike leaves the AT at the summit and follows a side trail 0.1 mile out to an overlook. The view is similar to the one from the ledges earlier in the hike, but it's more open and expansive.

At the north end of Nahmakanta Lake, whose Penobscot name suggests the lake is full of togue (lake trout), is a commercial camp on the site of Joe Francis's fishing camp, a famous Penobscot guide. Today the lake has only a carry-in boat launch, so you may see a canoe moving slowing through the water, but you will never hear a motorboat. From the lake you can see that Nesuntabunt Mountain has three summits—the hike crosses only the north one. The mountain's name means "three humps."

Climbing to the cliffs

Miles and Directions

0.0 Start at the southbound Appalachian Trail, 50 feet up the road from the parking area. There is a rough sign at the road and an official AT sign 100 feet down the trail.

0.6 The AT climbs gently to a cliff top with fine views across Nahmakanta Lake to Katahdin.

1.1 The AT crosses a wide, wooded ledge between the cliffs down to the lake and cliffs up to the summit of Nesuntabunt Mountain. The trail climbs, then skirts around to the north side of the mountain. There the AT climbs steeply through the woods to the summit. The southbound AT continues to the right; the hike turns left onto a side trail out to a cliff-top overlook.

1.2 From the overlook you have an expansive view across Nahmakanta Lake of Katahdin and beyond. To complete the hike, return the way you came.

2.4 Arrive back at the trailhead.

8 Nesuntabunt Mountain from the South

The Appalachian Trail follows the shore of Nahmakanta Lake, passing three beaches and a large spring. The trail climbs Nesuntabunt Mountain from the southeast through a gorge into the saddle between the north and middle peaks. Across the north peak, a side trail leads to a spectacular overlook high above Nahmakanta Lake with a view of Katahdin.

Start: Northbound Appalachian Trail, across Nahmakanta Stream Road from the parking area
Elevation gain: 2,203 feet
Distance: 9.4 miles out and back
Hiking time: About 5 hours
Difficulty: Strenuous
Season: June–Oct
Trail surface: Woodland path
Land status: Appalachian Trail corridor through Nahmakanta Public Land
Nearest town: Brownville
Other users: None
Water availability: Nahmakanta Lake, Prentiss Brook, Wadleigh Brook

Canine compatibility: Dogs must be under control at all times.
Fees and permits: Access fee paid at the Jo-Mary gatehouse
Maps: *DeLorme: Maine Atlas & Gazetteer:* Maps 42 and 50; USGS Nahmakanta Stream, Wadleigh Mountain, Rainbow Lake West
Trail contact: Nahmakanta Public Reserved Land; (207) 827-1818; maine.gov/nahmakanta
Amenities available: The hike passes a reliable spring and an AT lean-to.
Maximum grade: Climb from the lean-to to the summit averages 14% grade for 0.8 mile, with two short sections as steep as 25% grade.
Cell service: None

Finding the trailhead: From the bridge over the Pleasant River in Brownville, drive north on ME 11 for 15.6 miles. Turn left onto Jo-Mary Road; there is a large sign for Jo-Mary Campground at the intersection. Drive 0.1 mile to the gate; stop and pay fee. Drive 6 miles to a fork in the road; turn right, staying on Jo-Mary Road. Drive 9.9 miles, where you will pass the trailhead parking for Turtle Ridge and Tumbledown Dick Falls. Continue 4 miles to an intersection and turn right onto Wadleigh Pond Road. Drive 0.9 mile to Nahmakanta Stream Road; turn right and continue 1 mile. The road forks; bear right. Drive another 1.9 miles, passing the side road to the boat launch at the foot of Nahmakanta Lake. Just before Nahmakanta Stream Road crosses the AT and then Nahmakanta Stream, park in the lot on the right. The trailhead is the northbound AT, across the road from the parking area. Trailhead GPS: N45° 44.161' / W09° 06.209'

The Hike

The northbound AT follows Nahmakanta Stream for a short distance then cuts through the woods to the carry-in boat launch at the foot of the lake. The trail follows along the shore of the lake, passing two beaches and crossing two rocky knolls with views. You reach a short side trail to another beach and a good-size spring. Past

Waves rolling down Nahmakanta Lake, with Nesuntabunt Mountain in the distance

the spring, the trail turns inland from the shore and crosses Wadleigh Brook. In a short distance, you pass the lean-to.

Behind the lean-to, the trail climbs quickly into evergreens. A short climb brings you to the top of a dramatic cliff in the forest. You climb steadily along ledges and through mossy forest to an overlook with a partial view of Nahmakanta Lake and the mountains in Baxter State Park. This view is a teaser for what lies ahead.

The trail turns away from the overlook and climbs to a ridge, where a giant natural cairn sits. Descend off this ridge, then climb into a dramatic gorge with high cliffs. Past the cliffs, the trail climbs steadily up the wide saddle between two of Nesuntabunt's three peaks through a blanket of wildflowers beneath widely spaced hardwoods.

A short climb to the right brings you to the north peak. A marked side trail leads 500 feet to a dramatic overlook. You have an unobstructed view of Nahmakanta Lake and Katahdin in the distance. This route is much longer than the climb from the north to this point, but the interesting features along the way make it worth the extra work.

Nesuntabunt Mountain from the South

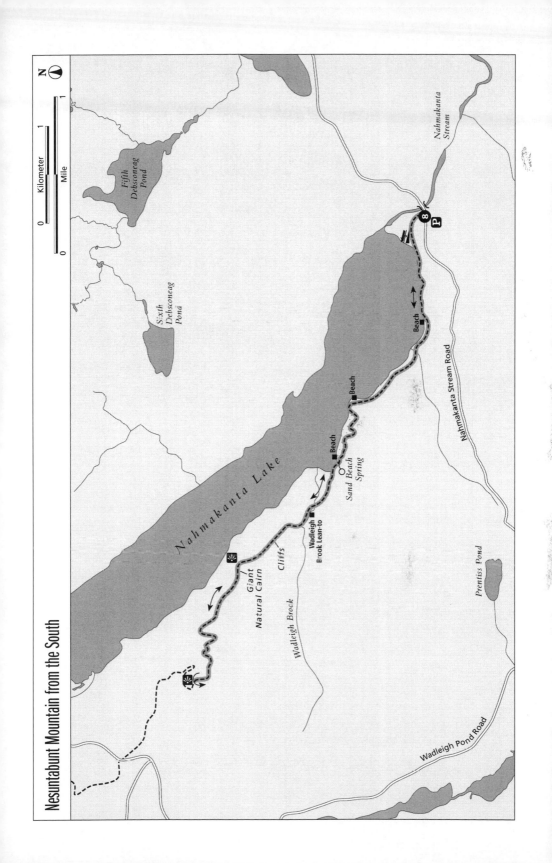

Katahdin from Nesuntabunt Mountain

Miles and Directions

0.0 Start from the AT northbound, across the road from the trailhead.

0.3 Cross through the woods to the boat launch and picnic area. The trail turns right, then left.

0.7 Reach a small beach on Nahmakanta Lake.

1.1 Cross over a small, rocky hill to Prentiss Brook.

1.6 The trail crosses a gravel beach.

2.3 Climb over a rocky hill to short, marked side trail that leads in 50 feet to Sand Beach Spring.

2.6 Hike through open hardwood forest. Cross Wadleigh Brook.

2.8 Pass the Wadleigh Brook Lean-to.

3.2 Climb steadily to high cliffs in the woods.

3.4 Pass an overlook. You can see Katahdin to the right through the trees.

3.5 Climb to a giant natural cairn.

4.0 Descend from the cairn, then climb to a gorge.

4.5 Switchback up cliffs onto a hardwood-covered saddle.

4.6 Turn right at the top of the saddle and climb to Nesuntabunt Mountain's north peak. Go straight onto the blue-blazed overlook trail.

4.7 The trail ends at an overlook of Nahmakanta Lake and Katahdin. To complete the hike, retrace your steps to the trailhead.

9.4 Arrive back at the trailhead.

9 Pollywog Falls and Crescent Pond

The north woods you hike through to get to the waterfalls are gorgeous. You hike around Crescent Pond and over a small spruce-covered hill. Upper Pollywog Falls is within sight of Pollywog Pond. It's a 20-foot drop down a seam in the granite bedrock. Lower Pollywog Falls drops 20 feet down a granite dam across the river into a large pool. A slab of granite overhangs the falls.

Start: Northbound Appalachian Trail from the crossing on Wadleigh Pond Road
Elevation gain: 831 feet
Distance: 4.0 miles out and back
Hiking time: 2–3 hours
Difficulty: Moderate
Season: Late May–Oct
Trail surface: Woodland path
Land status: Appalachian Trail corridor and Nahmakanta Public Reserved Land
Nearest town: Brownville
Other users: Hunters in season
Water availability: Crescent Pond

Canine compatibility: Dogs must be under control at all times.
Fees and permits: Access fee paid at Jo-Mary gatehouse
Maps: *DeLorme: Maine Atlas & Gazetteer:* Map 50; USGS Rainbow Lake West
Trail contact: Nahmakanta Public Reserved Land; (207) 941-4412; maine.gov/nahmakanta KI Jo-Mary Forest; (207) 435-6213; northmainewoods.org
Amenities available: None
Maximum grade: 19% in a very short section from the top of Lower Pollywog Falls to its base
Cell service: None

Finding the trailhead: From the bridge over the Pleasant River in Brownville on ME 11, drive north 15.7 miles. Turn left onto Jo-Mary Road at the Jo-Mary Campground sign. The gate where you pay the fee is 0.1 mile from ME 11. From the gate, drive 5.9 miles to a fork in the road; bear right onto Wadleigh Pond Road. At 11.4 miles from the gate, you will cross a stream and the Appalachian Trail. At 15.8 miles from the gate, you pass the Turtle Ridge Trail. At 19.7 miles from the gate, you come to a T intersection. Turn right, staying on Wadleigh Pond Road. At 20.6 miles from the first gate, the road bends left and a smaller road goes straight; bear left, staying on Wadleigh Pond Road. At 21.6 miles from the first gate, you will pass Nahmakanta Stream Road on the right. At 24.7 miles from the gate, pass Pollywog Pond Road. At 0.2 mile past the road, there will be a small, unmarked parking area on the left. Turn in here and park. The Appalachian Trail is 20 feet farther down the road. The hike follows the northbound AT on the west side of the road, next to the parking area. Trailhead GPS: N45° 45.809' / W69° 10.540'

The Hike

The Appalachian Trail climbs a small hill through a spruce forest. Nothing grows beneath the trees but moss and rocks. You descend gently to the shore of Crescent Pond. The trail loops around the pond, crossing multiple granite ledges with access to the picturesque pond. After you've walked about three-fourths of the way around, leave the AT and follow the Great Circle Trail, heading south. In a short distance

Upper Pollywog Falls

Crescent Pond

Lower Pollywog Falls

you'll cross Crescent Pond's narrow outlet stream and lose sight of the pond. Across the stream, go around a huge boulder then slab around the hill you climbed at the beginning of the hike.

Reach a marked junction. Turn right, staying on the Pollywog Trail and descend an old twitch trail. You'll be able to hear Lower Pollywog Falls. The trail levels out and crosses a ledge.

Turn right onto the Upper Falls Trail at the sign. This trail descends to the bouldery expanse at the waterfall. It's easiest to reach the falls by staying high and left on the rocks; you'll come out onto an open expanse of bedrock. Above you to the left, Pollywog Brook flows out of the pond. It drops through a rocky bed then leaps down a wide crack in the bedrock, falling 20 feet into a pool. This is one of the more picturesque waterfalls in Maine.

To visit Lower Falls, which is out of sight about 0.2 mile downstream, return to the Pollywog Trail. Turn left and then almost immediately left again onto the Lower Falls Trail. This trail wanders downstream. The last 200 feet to the pool at the base of Lower Pollywog Falls is very steep.

Lower Pollywog Falls drops 20 feet over exposed bedrock that crosses the stream. The falls are across the large pool against the cliff on the far side of the gorge. A huge slab of granite juts out of the hillside, hanging over the waterfall. If you don't mind swimming in water almost black from tannin, this is a good pool. Once you've enjoyed the waterfall, retrace your steps to the parking area.

Below Lower Pollywog Falls, the brook drops through a deep gorge. It's almost continuous whitewater to Rainbow Stream. The Appalachian Trail follows the brook high on the ridge, with some nice views of the gorge.

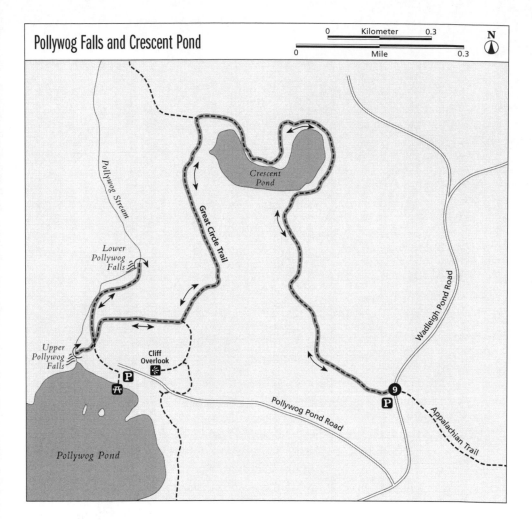

Pollywog Falls and Crescent Pond

Miles and Directions

0.0 Start on the northbound Appalachian Trail, on the west side of Wadleigh Pond Road.

0.5 Cross over a small hill to Crescent Pond.

1.1 Loop around Crescent Pond. Turn left onto the unsigned, blue-blazed Pollywog Trail.

1.5 Bear right at the intersection.

1.7 Turn right at a sign onto the Upper Falls Trail.

1.8 Reach Upper Pollywog Falls. To continue the hike, return to the Pollywog Trail.

1.9 Turn left, back onto the Pollywog Trail; almost immediately, turn left onto the Lower Falls Trail at a sign.

2.1 Reach the base of Lower Pollywog Falls. To complete the hike, return to the Pollywog Trail.

2.3 Turn left, back on the Pollywog Trail. Retrace your steps to the trailhead.

4.0 Arrive back at the trailhead.

10 Pollywog Falls and Cliffs

There are no open views from the cliffs, but they're still an interesting rock formation to hike up. The two Pollywog Falls are dramatic and quite different. Upper Falls drops almost directly out of Pollywog Pond down a granite face. When the water is high, this waterfall becomes three distinct falls. Lower Falls is a wide horsetail falls overhung by a cliff.

Start: Where the Great Circle Trail crosses Pollywog Pond Road, 200 feet east of the parking area
Elevation gain: 287 feet
Distance: 1.2-mile loop
Hiking time: About 1 hour
Difficulty: Easy
Season: June–Oct
Trail surface: Woodland path
Land status: Nahmakanta Public Reserved Land
Nearest town: Brownville
Other users: Hunters in season
Water availability: None
Canine compatibility: Dogs must be under control at all times.

Fees and permits: Access fee paid at the Jo-Mary gatehouse
Maps: *DeLorme: Maine Atlas & Gazetteer:* Map 50; USGS Rainbow Lake West
Trail contact: Nahmakanta Public Reserved Land; (207) 941-4412; maine.gov/nahmakanta KI Jo-Mary Forest; (207) 435-6213, northmainewoods.org
Amenities available: Picnic table on the shore of Pollywog Pond at the parking area
Maximum grade: 16% for 0.1 mile from the trailhead; 19% in a very short section from the top of Lower Pollywog Falls to its base
Cell service: None

Finding the trailhead: From the bridge over the Pleasant River in Brownville on ME 11, drive north 15.7 miles. Turn left onto Jo-Mary Road at the Jo-Mary Campground sign. The gate where you pay the fee is 0.1 mile from ME 11. From the gate, drive 5.9 miles to a fork in the road and bear right onto Wadleigh Pond Road. At 11.4 miles from the gate, you cross a stream and the Appalachian Trail. At 15.8 miles from the gate, you pass the Turtle Ridge Trail. At 19.7 miles from the gate, you come to a T intersection. Turn right, staying on Wadleigh Pond Road. At 20.6 miles from the first gate, the road bends left and a smaller road goes straight; bear left, staying on Wadleigh Pond Road. At 21.6 miles from the first gate, you will pass Nahmakanta Stream Road on the right. At 24.7 miles from the gate, turn left onto Pollywog Pond Road. Drive 0.2 mile to the parking area at the end of the road near the picnic area. Trailhead GPS: N45° 45.807' / W69° 11.087'

The Hike

The trail leaves Pollywog Pond Road and climbs almost immediately. The bulk of the cliffs is visible to your left through towering evergreens. Atop the cliffs, a side trail leads out to an overlook with a partial view of Pollywog Pond. The cliffs at your feet make giant steps down to the road below you. Use paths descend off the highest point where hikers explored the mossy rock face and tried to find more-open views.

Upper Pollywog Falls during high water

The Great Circle Trail continues off the cliffs through hardwoods a short distance to a junction. Turn left and hike downhill toward the waterfalls. Separate side trails leave the main trail on the same ledge to the waterfalls. Both are signed, but coming from this direction, you're likely to notice the sign for Upper Falls first, even though it's the second side trail.

The easiest way to reach Upper Pollywog Falls is to stay high and left when the trail reaches the ledges. When the water is high, there's a channel in the crack you first reach, and just to your right would be a pretty waterfall. Most of the year this channel is empty, making access to the falls easier. Upper Falls crashes down a seam in the granite dam that holds back Pollywog Pond. When the water is high, a second waterfall will be further to the right at the edge of this granite formation. The ledge you stand on slopes steeply down to the stream. By working downstream 100 feet, you can lower yourself to the stream level.

Partial view of Pollywog Pond from the cliffs

The side trail to Lower Falls is very different. It wanders through the mossy forest among boulders, out of sight of the stream. As the stream comes into view, the trail drops steeply, ending at the pool below the waterfall. Lower Falls drops across a ledge that spans the gorge. Cliffs on the far side overhang the stream.

Past the two side trails, it's a short, rocky descent to the road's end and the parking area. Make sure to walk out to the picnic area for a nice view of Pollywog Pond. You can often find ducks hanging around the rocks off to your right above the waterfall.

Miles and Directions

0.0 Start on the Great Circle Trail where it crosses Pollywog Pond Road, 200 feet east of the parking area. Follow the trail north of the road.

0.1 Turn left onto a side trail to cliff tops.

0.2 Reach cliff tops with a partial view of Pollywog Pond. Return to the Great Circle Trail.

0.3 Turn left, back on the Great Circle Trail.

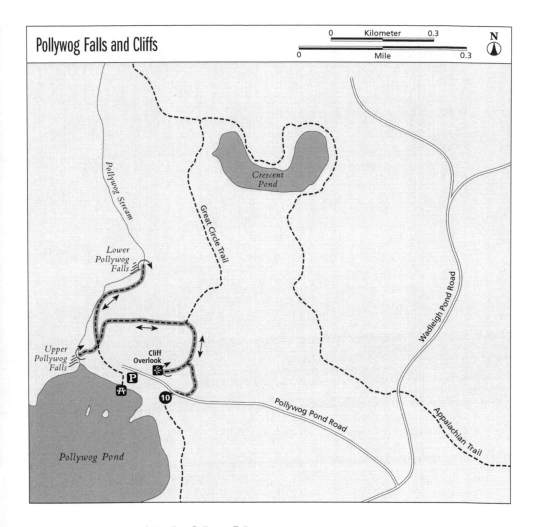

Pollywog Falls and Cliffs

0   Kilometer   0.3

0   Mile   0.3

N

0.4 Turn left onto the trail to Pollywog Falls.

0.5 Bear right onto the trail to Upper Pollywog Falls.

0.6 Descend onto and cross ledges to Upper Pollywog Falls. Return to the previous intersection.

0.7 At the intersection, bear left toward Lower Pollywog Falls.

0.9 Slab along a gorge, then descend to the base of Lower Pollywog Falls. Return to the previous intersection.

1.1 Bear left, away from the waterfalls.

1.2 Arrive back at the parking area.

11 Wadleigh Mountain from the North

Wadleigh Mountain rises west of Wadleigh and Musquash Ponds, across the valley from Nesuntabunt Mountain. The beginning of this hike is along the shore of Wadleigh Pond. Before climbing, you cross Female Brook on a very long log bridge. You'll pass through The Gateway and climb into a beautiful evergreen and boulder forest to reach the semi–open summit. Open ledges with views are less than 0.5 mile across the summit.

Start: Bridge over Wadleigh Outlet Stream
Elevation gain: 1,286 feet
Distance: 5.6 miles out and back
Hiking time: About 4 hours
Difficulty: Moderate
Season: June–Oct
Trail surface: Woodland path
Land status: Nahmakanta Public Reserved Land
Nearest town: Brownville
Other users: Hunters in season
Water availability: Wadleigh Pond and Female Brook
Canine compatibility: Dogs must be under control at all times.

Fees and permits: Access fee paid at the Jo-Mary gatehouse
Other maps: *DeLorme: The Maine Atlas & Gazetteer:* Map 42; USGS Wadleigh Mountain
Trail contact: Nahmakanta Public Reserved Land; (207) 941-4412; maine.gov/nahmakanta KI Jo-Mary Forest; (207) 435-6213; northmainewoods.org
Amenities available: Lean-to and tent site along Wadleigh Pond
Maximum grade: Consistent 10% climb from Female Brook to summit
Cell service: None

Finding the trailhead: Drive north on ME 11 out of Brownville for 15.7 miles. Turn left onto Jo-Mary Road (at the sign for Jo-Mary Campground) and drive 0.1 mile. Stop and pay the entrance fee. Continue on Jo-Mary Road another 6 miles; turn right, staying on Jo-Mary Road. Continue 16.2 miles. Pass the trailhead parking for the Turtle Ridge and Tumbledown Dick Trails. Continue another 3.9 miles. Turn right at three-way junction onto Wadleigh Pond Road and drive 3.7 miles. Turn left at the sign for Wadleigh Narrows campsites; drive downhill past the campsites to a parking area just before the bridge over Wadleigh Outlet Stream. The bridge is the trailhead. Trailhead GPS: N45° 45.023' / W69° 11.762'

The Hike

The hike begins by crossing Wadleigh Outlet on a stout bridge. You can see Wadleigh Pond upstream and Pollywog Pond downstream. The drop from one pond to the other is only 8 feet, so the stream's course is just riffles. In contrast, the drop into Wadleigh Pond is a pretty waterfall (with no trail to it), and the drop out of Pollywog Pond is a beautiful waterfall.

Across the bridge, you turn left off the roadbed (that you'll return to later) onto a trail that follows along the shore of Wadleigh Pond. The hike goes up the steps to the

Wadleigh Mountain's summit

lean-to (the trail continues along the pond a short distance to a tent site). Behind the lean-to, turn left, back onto the roadbed, and follow it.

Again, turn left off the roadbed onto a trail. Drop down to and cross Female Brook on a remarkable bridge—the longest log bridge I've seen in Maine. Follow Female Brook toward Wadleigh Pond, visible through the trees. Turn away from the lake and climb through hardwoods. The trail climbs steadily beside a tiny brook to a logging road. Across the logging road, you continue to follow the brook. The brook peters out where the trail crosses a knob. Above the knob, the trail reaches The Gateway, a band of exposed boulders you climb up between. Past The Gateway, the trail steepens as you climb into spruce on the summit ridge. The trail wanders across the summit ridge, climbing gently up steps of exposed mossy rock.

There used to be a tower on the semi-open summit. You can still see the remains of the bolts and plates that held it in place. There are no views from the summit. If you need a view, continue down across the summit a few tenths of a mile to open ledges.

Log bridge over Female Stream

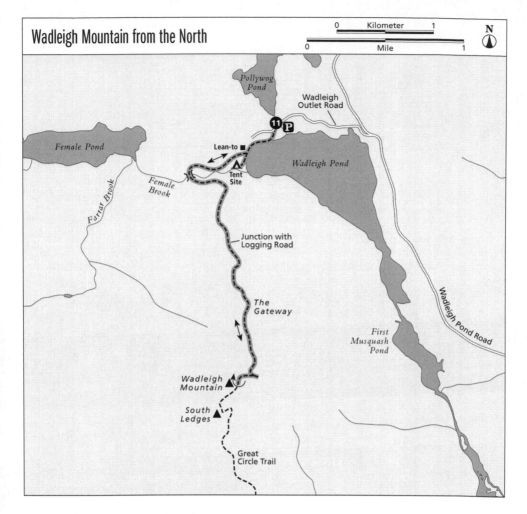

Wadleigh Mountain from the North

Map labels:
Pollywog Pond
Wadleigh Outlet Road
Female Pond
Lean-to
Wadleigh Pond
Tent Site
Female Brook
Farrar Brook
Junction with Logging Road
The Gateway
Wadleigh Pond Road
First Musquash Pond
Wadleigh Mountain
South Ledges
Great Circle Trail

Miles and Directions

0.0 Start by crossing the bridge over Wadleigh Outlet Stream.

0.4 The trail leaves the logging road and follows the shore of Wadleigh Pond to a lean-to. A side trail continues straight along the pond to a tent campsite. Turn left and pass the lean-to.

0.5 The trail turns left and rejoins the old logging road.

0.9 The trail leaves the logging road and crosses Female Brook on a bridge.

1.2 The trail begins climbing beside a small brook.

1.6 Cross a gravel road and continue to climb beside the brook.

2.1 Pass through a rock formation known as The Gateway.

2.8 Climb steadily to the semi-open but unmarked summit of Wadleigh Mountain. To complete the hike, retrace your steps to the trailhead.

5.6 Arrive back at the trailhead.

12 Wadleigh Mountain from the South

From the Katahdin View Trailhead, it's a long, gentle approach to Wadleigh Mountain. Past Third Musquash Pond, the trail climbs gently then steeply to open ledges with fine views. From there it's a short, interesting climb to the semi-open summit.

Start: Katahdin View Trailhead, at north end of the parking area
Elevation gain: 1,261 feet
Distance: 7.4 miles out and back
Hiking time: About 5 hours
Difficulty: Moderate
Season: June–Oct
Trail surface: Woodland path
Land status: Nahmakanta Public Reserved Land
Nearest town: Brownville
Other users: Hunters in season
Water availability: Third Musquash Pond
Canine compatibility: Dogs must be under control at all times.

Fees and permits: Access fee paid at the Jo-Mary gatehouse
Maps: *DeLorme: Maine Atlas & Gazetteer:* Map 42; USGS Wadleigh Mountain
Trail contact: Nahmakanta Public Reserved Land; (207) 941-4412; maine.gov/nahmakanta KI Jo-Mary Forest; (207) 435-6213; northmainewoods.org
Amenities available: None
Maximum grade: 12% for 0.9 mile on climb to summit, with four short climbs of 30% or greater
Cell service: None

Finding the trailhead: Drive north on ME 11 out of Brownville for 15.7 miles. Turn left onto Jo-Mary Road (at the sign for Jo-Mary Campground) and drive 0.1 mile. Stop and pay the entrance fee. Continue on Jo-Mary Road for another 6 miles; turn right, staying on Jo-Mary Road, and drive 16.2 miles. Pass the trailhead parking for the Turtle Ridge and Tumbledown Dick Trails. Continue another 3.9 miles. Turn left at the intersection onto Penobscot Pond Road and drive 1 mile uphill. Turn right into the parking area, just past a giant boulder sitting beside the road. The trailhead, marked with two signs, is at the north end of the parking area. Trailhead GPS. N45° 41.750' / W69° 10.013'

The Hike

The trail over Wadleigh Mountain is fairly new, so the trail bed isn't well-established. This means your hike will feel more like a ramble through the forest than a hike on a trail. The trail wanders through the mostly open hardwood forest interspersed with patches of dense evergreens. Where the evergreens are, there's bedrock near or at the surface. You pass one formation that looks like a huge whale breaking the surface. In another place, a cabin-sized boulder sits beside the trail.

A mile and half into the hike, you reach bedrock broken by a small stream that tumbles down the joint cracks in the rock. From below (if you bushwhack downstream), the formation almost looks constructed—large square blocks stacked neatly and finished with moss. The trail turns left and follows the brook upstream.

View from the ledges with Jo-Mary Mountain in the distance

There's a cleft with a small waterfall at its head, which the brook passes through. It's all very picturesque.

Farther upstream, the brook becomes marshy; the trail climbs away from the brook and wanders within sight of recent cutting. Eventually the stream becomes the marshy end of Third Musquash Pond. As you near the pond, an unmarked side trail leads a short distance to the marshy shore. A little farther on, a marked side trail leads to a campsite on the shore of the pond. You have a nice view of the low mountains across the water. At 0.25 mile past the campsite, another unmarked but obvious side trail leads 100 feet to the pond. From this point, you can see the shoulder of Wadleigh Mountain and the ledges the hike crosses.

The trail climbs gently away from the pond toward an obvious notch in Wadleigh Mountain. The trail steepens and goes straight up the cleft in the mountainside. As you near the top, the trail turns left and slabs around the mountain to a side trail that leads out onto the ledges. Be sure to hike all the way out the ledges. The first ledge offers only a partial view; to get an open view, you have to follow the trail through a small stand of trees. From the open ledges, you have a spectacular view south and west.

Third Musquash Pond

At the side trail to the lower ledges, the trail turns right and climbs steeply for a short distance to a second side trail out onto the upper ledges. Above the ledges, the trail turns back east and climbs to the summit through mossy spruce forest. You climb several ledges in the woods to reach the semi-open summit. Until recently, there was a tower here. You can still see the bolts sticking out of the bedrock.

Miles and Directions

0.0   Start at the Katahdin View Trailhead, at the north end of the parking area.

1.5   The trail wanders through the woods to a waterfall. The trail makes a sharp left, follows the brook upstream, then crosses it.

2.2   Climb away from the brook and pass some cut-over areas on the right. The trail drops back down to the brook. An obvious but unmarked side trail on the left leads 100 feet to the brook.

2.3   Pass a side trail on the left that leads 100 feet to a campsite on the shore of Third Musquash Pond.

2.5   A side trail leads 100 feet to Third Musquash Pond. There's a view of the ledges on Wadleigh Mountain.

Bridge over Musquash Brook

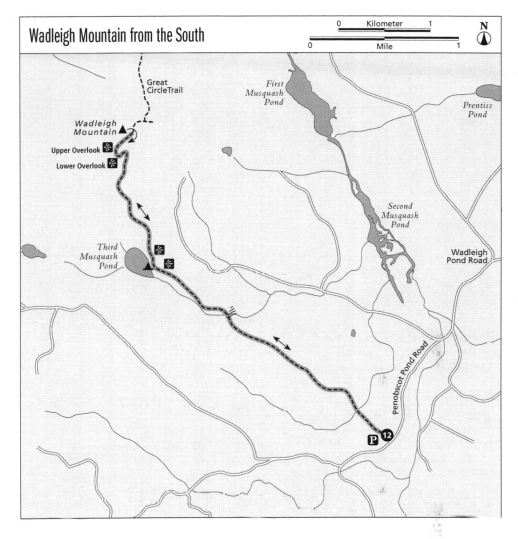

Wadleigh Mountain from the South

3.5 The trail wanders through the woods then climbs steadily. A side trail leads to open ledges with fine views. Make sure to continue past the first ledge, which has only partial views.

3.6 Climb steeply past a side trail to ledges to a second side trail to the upper ledges.

3.7 The trail climbs in fits and starts to the semi-open, unmarked summit. To complete the hike, retrace your steps to the trailhead.

7.4 Arrive back at the trailhead.

13 Musquash Ledges

There are lots of ledge falls in Maine, but Musquash Ledges is the longest one. The stream tumbles down ledges for more than 0.25 mile, losing nearly 100 feet in elevation. Sections of the hike are on the bedrock ledges beside the stream. The woods beside the ledges are full of moss-covered boulders and wildflowers in season.

Start: Trailhead across the road from the parking area
Elevation gain: 114 feet
Distance: 0.9-mile loop
Hiking time: About 1 hour
Difficulty: Easy
Season: June–Oct
Trail surface: Woodland path and bedrock ledges
Land status: Nahmakanta Public Reserved Land
Nearest town: Brownville
Other users: Hunters in season
Water availability: Musquash Stream

Canine compatibility: Dogs must be under control at all times.
Fees and permits: Access fee paid at the Jo-Mary gatehouse
Maps: DeLorme: Maine Atlas & Gazetteer: Map 42; USGS Wadleigh Mountain
Trail contact: Nahmakanta Public Reserved Land; (207) 941-4412; maine.gov/nahmakanta
KI Jo-Mary Forest; (207) 435-6213; northmainewoods.org
Amenities available: None
Maximum grade: 5.5% climbing beside ledges for 0.2 mile
Cell service: None

Finding the trailhead: Drive north on ME 11 out of Brownville for 15.7 miles. Turn left onto Jo-Mary Road (at the sign for Jo-Mary Campground) and drive 0.1 mile. Stop and pay the entrance fee. Continue on Jo-Mary Road for another 6 miles. Turn right, staying on Jo-Mary Road, and continue 16.2 miles. Pass the trailhead parking for the Turtle Ridge and Tumbledown Dick Trails. Continue another 3.MAP: Bypasses. Turn left at the intersection onto Penobscot Pond Road and drive 1 mile uphill. Turn right into the Katahdin View Trailhead parking area, just past a giant boulder sitting beside the road. The signed trailhead is across the road. Trailhead GPS: N45° 41.747' / W69° 09.985'

The Hike

"Musquash" is the Penobscot word for "muskrat." I'm doubting many muskrats spend time on the ledges themselves, but I'm sure they're common in the marshy stream and ponds downstream from Musquash Ledges. The stream flows out of Harding Pond near the Turtle Ridge west trailhead. It's not a large pond, but the stream maintains good water flow even in summer. This means you don't need to do this hike in spring to enjoy it.

The hike to the base of the ledges is through a very mossy evergreen forest—a good place to find trilliums in the spring. As you near the stream, the boulders get larger and more jumbled. There's a large pool at the base of the lowest slide on the ledges. The trail loops around the pool and emerges onto the ledges beside the stream.

As you climb beside Musquash Stream, the trail crosses ledge—sometimes requiring jumping over side channels—and scoots into the woods. Back and forth you go

Musquash Ledges

Approaching the base of the ledges

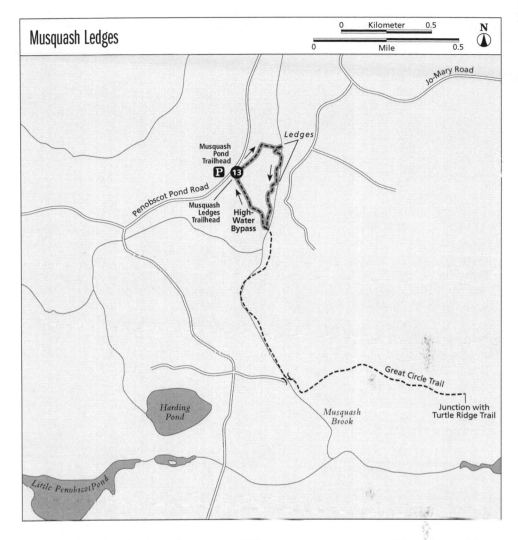

as you climb beside the rushing water. This gives you great views of the various slides and falls on the ledges.

Above the ledges, you follow the stream before reaching the High Water Bypass. Turn right onto it and follow it back to the trailhead.

Miles and Directions

0.0 Start at the Musquash Ledges Trailhead, across the road from the parking area. In 100 feet, bear left at the junction.

0.2 The trail wanders through the bouldery woods to the base of Musquash Ledges.

0.7 The trail follows the ledges upstream, sometimes in the woods and sometimes on the ledges. Leave the ledges and reach an intersection. Turn right.

0.9 Arrive back at the trailhead.

14 Tumbledown Dick Falls via the Appalachian Trail

The hike along Nahmakanta Stream is mostly through towering evergreens. The stream rushes by on its way to Pemadumcook Lake. The easy hike from there to Tumbledown Dick Falls is mostly through hardwoods. A side trail leads down to the base of the falls through a boulder descent. Flanked by high granite cliffs, the falls is one of the region's highest. The trail continues past the side trail to the top of the waterfall.

Start: Southbound AT between parking area and bridge over Nahmakanta Stream
Elevation gain: 731 feet
Distance: 4.0 miles out and back
Hiking time: About 2 hours
Difficulty: Easy
Season: June–Oct
Trail surface: Woodland path
Land status: Appalachian Trail and Nahmakanta Public Reserved Land
Nearest town: Brownville
Other users: Hunters in season
Water availability: Nahmakanta Stream
Canine compatibility: Dogs must be under control at all times.

Fees and permits: Access fee paid at the Jo-Mary gatehouse
Maps: *DeLorme: Maine Atlas & Gazetteer:* Map 42; USGS Nahmakanta Stream
Trail contact: Nahmakanta Public Reserved Land; (207) 941-4412; maine.gov/nahmakanta KI Jo-Mary Forest; (207) 435-6213; northmainewoods.org
Amenities available: None
Maximum grade: 18% descent from main trail to base of falls; consistent 6% climb from Nahmakanta Stream to Tumbledown Dick Falls
Cell service: None

Finding the trailhead: From the bridge over the Pleasant River in Brownville on ME 11, drive north 15.7 miles. Turn left onto Jo-Mary Road at the Jo-Mary Campground sign. The gate where you pay the fee is 0.1 mile from ME 11. From the gate, drive 5.9 miles to a fork in the road and bear right onto Wadleigh Pond Road. At 11.4 miles from the gate, you will cross a stream and the Appalachian Trail. At 15.8 miles from the gate, you pass the Turtle Ridge Trail. At 19.7 miles from the gate, you come to a T intersection. Turn right, staying on Wadleigh Pond Road. At 20.6 miles from the first gate, the road bends left and a smaller road goes straight; bear left, staying on Wadleigh Pond Road. At 21.6 miles from the gate, turn right onto Nahmakanta Stream Road and drive 1 mile. The road bears right at a fork. Drive another 2 miles, passing the side road to the boat launch at the foot of Nahmakanta Lake. At 0.1 mile beyond the side road, park on the right just before Nahmakanta Stream Road crosses the Appalachian Trail and then Nahmakanta Stream. The trailhead is the southbound AT, on the same side of the road as the parking area. Trailhead GPS: N45° 44.162' W69° 06.206'

The Hike

Tumbledown Dick was a nickname for Richard Cromwell—who ruled Great Britain for nine months in 1658–59. He was given the nickname because he fell from power so quickly after becoming Lord Protector upon his father's death. What Cromwell's

Tumbledown Dick Falls

On the AT along Nahmakanta Stream

failed reign has to do with a waterfall in northern Maine is a mystery. Maybe it's the way the stream leaps off a high granite ledge and plunges more than 70 feet into a wide, shallow pool.

The hike begins by following Nahmakanta Stream as it rushes toward Pemadumcook Lake. You roller-coaster over side hills covered with towering evergreens as the stream crashes down its rocky bed. After a mile, you turn right onto the Tumbledown Dick Falls Trail and climb away from the stream and the evergreens.

As you hike along, you'll hear Tumbledown Dick Falls before you catch a glimpse of it through the trees. You then descend into a notch in the bedrock and turn left onto a marked side trail. This trail descends steeply through boulders to the base of the waterfall. High cliffs surround the rocky meadow the stream passes through below the falls. The waterfall is where the cliffs on the two sides comes together. It's one of Maine's more dramatic waterfalls, and I was so enamored on my first visit that I almost stepped on a beaver. My attention was drawn away from the waterfall by an odd clicking noise. I stopped, my foot hovering a few feet off the ground. I looked down: I was about to step on a large beaver, expressing its displeasure by clicking its teeth. I stepped back, and it hurried away into the stream.

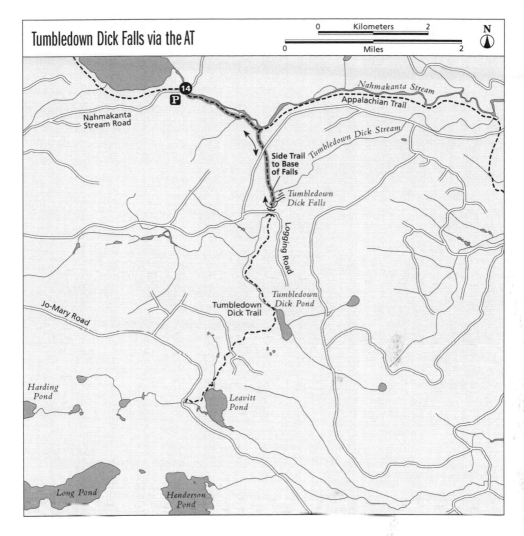

0   Kilometers   2

0   Miles   2

N

Before heading back to the trailhead, you can follow Tumbledown Dick Falls Trail north past the side trail a short distance to the top of the waterfall.

Miles and Directions

0.0   Start on the southbound AT, just west of the bridge over Nahmakanta Stream.

1.0   Roller-coaster beside Nahmakanta Stream through open evergreen forest. Turn right onto Tumbledown Dick Falls Trail at a sign.

1.9   Climb gently through hardwoods. Turn left onto a marked side trail.

2.0   Descend steeply through boulders to the base of Tumbledown Dick Falls. To complete the hike, retrace your steps to the trailhead. (**Option:** After returning to the Tumbledown Dick Falls Trail, turn left and climb 0.1 mile to the top of the waterfall before returning.)

4.0   Arrive back at the trailhead.

15 Tumbledown Dick Falls via Leavitt Pond

This hike to Tumbledown Dick Falls passes two remote ponds; follows Tumbledown Dick Stream as it, well, tumbles down into the Penobscot River valley; and ends at one of the most scenic waterfalls in Maine. The trail passes right next to the rock-choked head of the falls, where it plunges more than 60 feet into a pool. A side trail leads down a steep slope to the base of the falls.

Start: Turtle Ridge East parking area
Distance: 7.9 miles out and back
Hiking time: 3–5 hours
Difficulty: Strenuous because of the distance
Season: Best May–Oct
Trail surface: Woodland path
Land status: Nahmakanta Public Reserved Land
Nearest town: Greenville
Other users: Hunters in season
Water availability: Leavitt and Tumbledown Dick Ponds, Tumbledown Dick Stream

Canine compatibility: Dogs must be under control at all times.
Fees and permits: No fees or permits required
Maps: *DeLorme: Maine Atlas & Gazetteer:* Map 42; USGS Nahmakanta Stream
Trail contact: Nahmakanta Public Reserved Land; (207) 941-4412; maine.gov/nahmakanta
Amenities available: None
Maximum grade: 15% descent from top of falls to bottom for 0.2 mile
Cell service: None

Finding the trailhead: From the bridge over the Pleasant River in Brownville on ME 11, drive north 15.7 miles. Turn left onto Jo-Mary Road at the Jo-Mary Campground sign. The gate where you pay the fee is 0.1 mile from ME 11. From the gate, drive 5.9 miles to a fork in the road and bear right onto Wadleigh Pond Road. At 11.4 miles from the gate, you will cross a stream and the Appalachian Trail. At 14.1 miles from the gate, you pass another gate, which is remotely controlled from the gate where you paid your fee. At 15.8 miles from the first gate (2.7 miles past the second gate), you reach the trailhead parking, on the left. The trailhead is 275 feet farther up the road, on the opposite side from the parking area at a sign and rock piles. Trailhead GPS: N45° 41.100' / W69° 06.189'

The Hike

The Tumbledown Dick Trail descends through a mostly beech forest to Leavitt Pond. A side trail leads to a campsite to the shore of the pond. You can often find ducks or loons bobbing in the water here. Many days, the only people you'll see on this hike are anglers out in Leavitt Pond.

From Leavitt Pond the trail wanders through a broken landscape of bedrock ridges and old overgrown cuts. You walk in and out of dry, scratchy pine stands and aromatic hardwood lowlands—through blueberries and knee-high ferns and squishy bogs.

The trail drops down off a final granite ledge and follows a cliff down through scattered boulders to Tumbledown Dick Pond. A side trail leads out to the pond near

Top of Tumbledown Dick Falls

Tumbledown Dick Stream above the falls

the rock- and deadfall-choked north end, where Tumbledown Dick Stream begins its tumultuous run to Nahmakanta Stream.

The trail follows the stream, which is usually out of sight through the thick underbrush but always within earshot. Eventually the trail doglegs right and climbs a gentle sidehill. The stream drops away. From the west, Dead Brook flows into Tumbledown Dick Stream, almost doubling its flow.

The trail descends off the sidehill to the stream and ends at a logging road. Turn left and cross the stream on the road—a beautiful deadwater is visible around a rocky bend downstream. Across the bridge, the trail continues downstream along the deadwater.

The trail crosses a series of exposed bedrock slabs, several of which jut into the stream. Then the trail passes through a boulder choke at the head of the falls. Standing on the boulders, you can see the stream—choked down to only a few feet across— leap out over the rocks and drop 70 feet. A dark pool nestled against high black cliffs catches the water.

The trail turns away from the stream and descends to a junction. Straight ahead leads to the Appalachian Trail. The side trail to the right descends a wide chimney to the base of the waterfall. You can take time to explore the small meadow, trying to find the best view of Tumbledown Dick Falls and the cliffs.

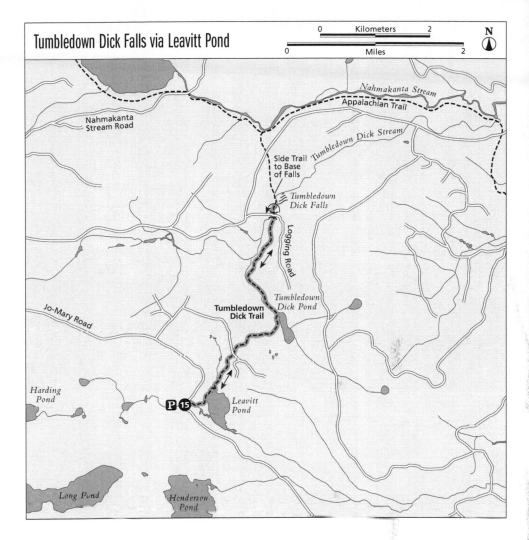

One day, when I was doing just that, I almost stepped on a beaver chewing on a downed birch tree at the edge of the pool. We both froze, looking into each other's eyes. Then the beaver turned and slipped into the water. A few seconds later it surfaced and slapped its tail, letting me know what it thought of my intrusion into its peaceful world.

Miles and Directions

0.0 Start from the sign at the east side of the Turtle Ridge East parking area, and walk northeast on Jo-Mary Road.

0.1 Turn right onto the Tumbledown Dick Trail at the sign and cairns.

0.6 A side trail leads 100 feet through a campsite to the shore of Leavitt Pond.

Tumbledown Dick Falls

2.0 The trail crosses several rocky ridges and old cuts before dropping down to Tumbledown Dick Pond. A side trail leads 100 feet through a campsite to the shore of the pond.

3.6 The trail comes out onto a logging road. Turn left and cross Tumbledown Dick Stream. Across the bridge, turn right at the sign, back onto the Tumbledown Dick Trail.

3.8 The trail follows Tumbledown Dick Stream toward the falls. A very short trail leads to the top of the falls.

3.9 Arrive at a marked junction. Straight ahead is the Appalachian Trail; turn right and descend to the bottom of Tumbledown Dick Falls.

4.0 Reach the bottom of the falls. To complete the hike, return the way you came.

7.9 Arrive back at the trailhead.

16 Turtle Ridge from the West

This fairly long hike explores a granite landscape of cliffs and ponds. There is one of the best views of Katahdin along the Henderson Pond Trail, and fine views of the mountains to the south and west from Turtle Ridge. The remote ponds the hike passes are home to loons and other waterbirds and visited by moose. The hike also offers some of the best fall foliage in Maine.

Start: Turtle Ridge west trailhead parking area at the end of Loop Pond Road
Distance: 9.9-mile lollipop
Elevation gain: 1,557 feet
Hiking time: About 6 hours
Difficulty: Strenuous because of the length
Season: Best May–Oct
Trail surface: Woodland path
Land status: Nahmakanta Public Reserved Land
Nearest town: Greenville
Other users: Hunters in season
Water availability: Stream near trailhead; several ponds along the hike
Canine compatibility: Dogs must be under control at all times.

Fees and permits: No fees or permits required
Maps: *DeLorme: Maine Atlas & Gazetteer:* Map 42; USGS Nahmakanta Stream and Wadleigh Mountain
Trail contact: Nahmakanta Public Reserved Land; (207) 941-4412; maine.gov/nahmakanta
Amenities available: Campsite with privy and picnic table on Sing Sing Pond
Maximum grade: Climb from Sing Sing Pond to the shoulder of Turtle Ridge is 8% for 0.9 mile; climb from junction with trail to east trailhead to clifftop overlook is 10% for 0.5 mile.
Cell service: None

Finding the trailhead: From the blinking light in Greenville, drive north on Lily Bay Road 18.9 miles. Just past Kokadjo, where the pavement ends, bear left onto Sias Hill Road and drive 1.6 miles. Turn right onto Smithtown Road and drive 3.6 miles. Turn left onto Penobscot Pond Road. There is a blue sign at the intersection for Nahmakanta Reserved Land. Continue 4 miles and bear left at the large Appalachian Mountain Club (AMC) sign. Drive 2.7 miles and bear right at an intersection. Continue 1.7 miles and turn left at an intersection onto Nahmakanta Road. Another blue sign directs you toward the Nahmakanta Reserved Land. Drive 1.4 miles, passing Penobscot Pond to the boundary of Nahmakanta Reserved Land. Continue 1 mile and bear right. (*Note:* On your return trip, this intersection might be confusing.) Drive 0.6 mile; turn right onto Loop Pond Road and continue for 1 mile. Trailhead parking is on the right, just before the gate across the road. The trailhead is the sign at the south end of the parking area. Trailhead GPS: N45° 40.916' / W69° 10.006'

The Hike

The Turtle Ridge hike skirts several ponds, crosses ridges with fine views, and passes through several different forest and habitat types. But what is constant along the entire 9.9 miles is the granite. Turtle Ridge and the other hills the trails cross are granite mounds with exposed bedrock and cliff faces; the ponds are overlooked by granite

Turtle Ridge across Sing Sing Pond

cliffs, their shores dotted with boulders. The forest floor is littered with boulders, some as big as a house. Everywhere you step and look, there's granite.

You don't reach this granite landscape until you turn onto the Turtle Ridge Trail and cross Sing Sing Pond's outlet stream. You then wind among large fern-covered boulders and pines to the shore of the pond. A granite shelf sticks out into the pond where you can rest, watch for loons, or swim in the cool water. (**Note:** Don't sit with your feet hanging in the water for too long—you'll attract leeches.)

Turtle Ridge is across Sing Sing Pond, its three humps visible. The westernmost hump is tree covered; the middle has a large granite cliff; the easternmost hump is a bare, rounded summit. The trail passes over each hump from west to east. Between the humps the trail drops and crosses behind the ridge. The view across Sing Sing Pond and the mixed lowland forest comes alive with color in the fall. Spring employs a subtler palette as the maples appear red from their flowers and the new leaves on the beech, birch, and ash trees appear almost lime green, all contrasting with the dark spruce and fir. On the horizon to the southwest are a line of mountains anchored in the east by Big Boardman Mountain; to the west are the Lily Bay Mountains. In the middle, keeping its snow cover late into spring, is White Cap Mountain.

The trail drops down off Turtle Ridge and wanders through the woods past Hedgehog Pond to Rabbit Pond. The trail crosses an exposed granite ledge that acts as a dam, holding back Rabbit Pond. The outlet stream slides across the

View from Turtle Ridge

granite and disappears into the woods. From Rabbit Pond its a short, rocky climb to an intersection.

A cairn holds a trail junction sign pointing to Henderson and Rabbit Ponds. The hike climbs toward Henderson Pond through spruce to a cliff top. From the cliffs is one of the best views of Katahdin. The mountain rises in the middle distance across rolling green hills dotted with ponds. At your feet are blueberries and wintergreen edged with moss and gray-green lichen.

Beyond the cliffs, the trail follows a spine of granite, skirting the hilltop. A side trail to an overlook of Henderson Pond goes out to a granite ridgetop but offers only very limited views. The best way to see Henderson Pond is to continue the hike, dropping down to the north shore of the pond, where you can walk out to the rocky shore and look for loons and other waterbirds. Across the pond rises Jo-Mary Mountain; at nearly 3,000 feet, it is the highest in the neighborhood but has no marked trail to its wooded summit.

The trail climbs gently away from Henderson Pond on a granite ridge that is drier than the woods so far on the hike. Here scratchy lichen grows on and around the boulders instead of moss. The trail passes Long Pond, although you can't see the pond or get to it. As the trail approaches some very mossy cliffs, it winds between boulders and then descends on steps. The trail wanders among granite beneath the cliff then ends at the Rabbit Pond Cutoff and Sing Sing Pond Trail. The Sing Sing Pond Trail follows a stream past a marshy pond in a low area, then follows an old woods road past Sing Sing Pond. This section is both moosey and very buggy. A campsite on the south shore of the pond offers views of Turtle Ridge.

Rabbit Pond Outlet

Miles and Directions

0.0 Start from the Turtle Ridge west trailhead.

0.1 Walk past the gate and cross the bridge over Musquash Stream. Follow Loop Pond Road south to the trail on the left.

1.1 Turn left onto the Turtle Ridge Trail. After crossing the outlet stream of Sing Sing Pond, the trail winds among large boulders and comes close to Sing Sing Pond. A short unmarked trail leads out to the pond, where there are boulders at its edge. This is a good spot to rest, swim, and watch for loons and moose. There are fine views across the pond of the three humps of Turtle Ridge.

1.9 Climb steadily to a junction with the Great Circle Trail. Continue straight on the Turtle Ridge Trail.

2.2 The Turtle Ridge Trail climbs up the west end of Turtle Ridge. The first summit hump is wooded, with only limited views. The second hump is open, and the trail passes across a high cliff top with views across Sing Sing Pond to White Cap and other mountains to the south.

2.3 The trail turns north from the cliffs and crosses the ridge. From the back of the ridge, there are limited views north of Katahdin. The trail then emerges onto the open summit of the third hump of Turtle Ridge, with unrestricted views in every direction except north.

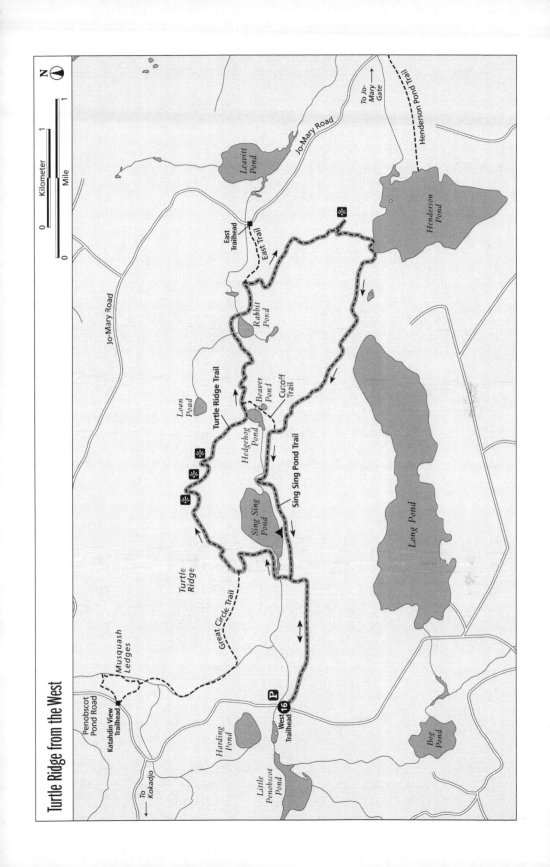

Turtle Ridge from the West

3.1 The trail descends off Turtle Ridge and skirts below some cliffs then crosses through the woods to Hedgehog Pond. Where the Turtle Ridge Trail makes a left turn, a short, unmarked side trail leads to the pond.

3.2 Junction with the Rabbit Pond Cutoff. Continue straight on the Turtle Ridge Trail toward Rabbit Pond. (**Option:** Take the Rabbit Pond Cutoff 0.2 mile to the Sing Sing Trail, making the hike 5.5 miles.)

4.2 The Turtle Ridge Trail crosses a spine of granite then comes to Rabbit Pond. The trail crosses exposed granite bedrock at the east end of Rabbit Pond. The pond's outlet stream flows over the rock and disappears into the woods.

4.6 The trail continues across the granite, climbing to the junction with the Henderson Pond Trail. Turn right onto the Henderson Pond Trail. (The east trailhead is 0.5 mile to the left.)

5.1 The Henderson Pond Trail climbs through a spruce forest to the top of a cliff with fine views to the north of Katahdin.

5.5 Beyond the cliffs, the trail turns south and follows a granite spine and then woods toward Henderson Pond. A marked side trail goes 0.1 mile to an overlook of the pond, but the views are mostly screened by trees.

6.0 The trail skirts the west edge of Henderson Pond (an unmarked trail leads to the pond). Across the pond, where you can often see loons, rises Jo-Mary Mountain.

7.6 The trail climbs a low, rocky ridge beyond Henderson Pond. Long Pond is to your south, unseen down the steep slope. There is no access to Long Pond on this hike. Past Long Pond, the trail drops down the edge of jumbled cliffs and then along their bottom to intersect the Rabbit Pond Cutoff. To continue the hike, turn left onto the Sing Sing Pond Trail.

8.0 The Sing Sing Pond Trail passes a small, marshy pond; an unmarked trail leads to a large boulder at its edge.

8.8 The Sing Sing Pond Trail follows a stream, then comes out onto an old woods road. The trail skirts the east side of Sing Sing Pond, visible through the trees. This section tends to be very buggy, but it offers the possibility of a moose sighting. Arrive back at the junction with the Turtle Ridge Trail. Continue straight, retracing your steps to the trailhead.

9.9 Arrive back at the trailhead.

17 Turtle Ridge from the East

This fairly long hike explores a granite landscape of cliffs and ponds. There is one of the best views of Katahdin along the Henderson Pond Trail, and fine views of the mountains to the south and west from Turtle Ridge. The remote ponds the hike passes are home to loons and other waterbirds and visited by moose. The hike also offers some of the best fall foliage in Maine.

Start: Turtle Ridge east trailhead, 275 feet south of the parking area across the bridge

Distance: 8.6-mile loop

Elevation gain: 1,556 feet

Hiking time: 5–6 hours

Difficulty: Moderate

Season: May–Oct

Trail surface: Woodland path

Land status: Nahmakanta Public Reserved Land

Nearest town: Brownville

Other users: Hunting is allowed on Maine Reserved Lands.

Water availability: Stream near trailhead; several ponds along the hike

Canine compatibility: Dogs must be under control at all times.

Fees and permits: Access fee paid at the Jo-Mary gatehouse

Maps: *DeLorme: Maine Atlas & Gazetteer:* Map 42; USGS Nahmakanta Stream and Wadleigh Mountain

Trail contact: Nahmakanta Public Reserved Land; (207) 941-4412; maine.gov/nahmakanta KI Jo-Mary Forest; (207) 435-6213; northmainewoods.org

Amenities available: Campsite with privy and picnic table on Sing Sing Pond

Maximum grade: 10% climb from east trailhead to cliff-top overlook in 1 mile; climb from Sing Sing Pond to shoulder of Turtle Ridge at 8% grade for 0.9 mile

Cell service: None

Finding the trailhead: From the bridge over the Pleasant River in Brownville on ME 11, drive north 15.7 miles. Turn left onto Jo-Mary Road at the Jo-Mary Campground sign. The gate where you pay the fee is 0.1 mile from ME 11. From the gate, drive 5.9 miles to a fork in the road. Turn right, staying on Jo-Mary Road. At 11.4 miles from the gate, you will cross a stream and the Appalachian Trail. At 15.8 miles from the gate, you reach the trailhead parking, on the left. The trailhead is 275 feet down the road the way you came, on the same side as the parking lot. Trailhead GPS: N45° 41.028' / W69° 06.243'

The Hike

The Turtle Ridge hike skirts several ponds, crosses ridges with fine views, and passes through several different forest and habitat types. But what is constant along the entire 8.6 miles is the granite. Turtle Ridge and the other hills the trails cross are granite mounds with exposed bedrock and cliff faces; the ponds are overlooked by granite cliffs, their shores dotted with boulders. The forest floor is littered with boulders, some as big as a house. Everywhere you step and look there is granite.

Katahdin from cliffs

The hike begins by winding through a spruce forest with moss-covered boulders of every size. A stream, unseen, tumbles down its rocky course, heading toward Leavitt Pond. The trail climbs gently to an irregular expanse of granite bedrock. The spruce forest is edged with blueberries and huckleberries that turn fiery red in the fall, contrasting with the rough, gray granite and dark spruce. A cairn holds a trail junction sign pointing to Henderson and Rabbit Ponds. The hike climbs toward Henderson Pond through spruce to a cliff top. From the cliffs is one of the best views of Katahdin. The mountain rises in the middle distance across rolling green hills dotted with ponds. At your feet are blueberries and wintergreen edged with moss and gray-green lichen. Beyond the cliffs, the trail follows a spine of granite, skirting the hilltop.

The side trail to an overlook of Henderson Pond goes out to a granite ridgetop that offers only limited views. The best way to see Henderson Pond is to continue the hike, dropping down to the north shore of the pond, where you can walk out to the rocky shore and look for loons and other waterbirds. Across the pond rises Jo-Mary Mountain; at nearly 3,000 feet, it is the highest in the neighborhood but has no trail to its wooded summit.

The trail climbs gently away from Henderson Pond on a granite ridge that is drier than the woods so far on the hike. Here scratchy lichen grows on and around the boulders instead of moss. The trail passes Long Pond, although you cannot see the pond or get to it. As the trail approaches some very mossy cliffs, it winds between boulders and then descends on steps. The trail wanders among granite beneath the cliff then ends at the Rabbit Pond Cutoff and Sing Sing Pond Trails. The Sing Sing Pond Trail follows a stream past a marshy pond in a low area, then follows an old woods road past Sing Sing Pond. This section is both moosey and very buggy. Access to Sing Sing Pond along this section is at the campsite.

The Turtle Ridge Trail crosses Sing Sing Pond's outlet stream then winds among large fern-covered boulders and pines to the shore of the pond. A granite shelf sticks out into the pond where you can rest, watch for loons, or swim in the cool water. (**Note:** Don't sit with your feet hanging in the water for too long—you'll attract leeches.)

Turtle Ridge is across Sing Sing Pond, its three humps visible. The westernmost hump is tree covered; the middle has a large granite cliff; the easternmost has a bare, rounded summit. The trail passes over each hump from west to east. Between the humps the trail drops and crosses behind the ridge with limited views of Katahdin to the north, especially when the trees have no leaves. The view across Sing Sing Pond and the mixed lowland forest comes alive with color in the fall. Spring employs a subtler palette as the maples appear red from their flowers and the new leaves on the beech, birch, and ash trees appear almost lime green, all contrasting with the dark spruce and fir. On the horizon to the southwest are a line of mountains anchored in the east by Big Boardman Mountain; to the west are the Lily Bay Mountains. In the middle, keeping its snow cover late into spring, is White Cap Mountain.

Ledges near the east trailhead

The trail drops down off Turtle Ridge and wanders through the woods past Hedgehog Pond to Rabbit Pond. The trail crosses an exposed granite ledge that acts as a dam, holding back Rabbit Pond. The outlet stream slides across the granite and disappears into the woods. From Rabbit Pond its a short, rocky climb to the first intersection you passed, closing the loop of the hike and ending a day exploring this granite landscape.

Miles and Directions

0.0   Start from the Turtle Ridge east trailhead, 275 feet south on the road from the parking area.

0.5   The trail winds through a boulder-filled forest then climbs an open granite area, where the trail forks. The Turtle Ridge Trail goes to the right (that will be where the hike ends). Take the Henderson Pond Trail to the left.

1.0   The Henderson Pond Trail climbs through a spruce forest to the top of a cliff with fine views to the north of Katahdin.

1.4   Beyond the cliffs, the trail turns south and follows a granite spine and then woods toward Henderson Pond. A marked side trail goes 0.1 mile to an overlook of the pond, but the views are mostly screened by trees.

Turtle Ridge from the East

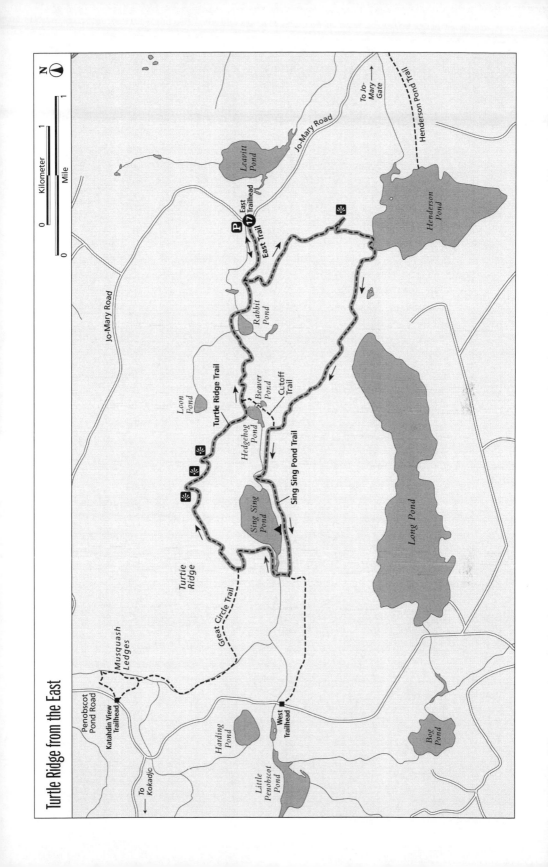

1.9 The trail skirts the west edge of Henderson Pond; an unmarked trail leads to the pond. Across the pond, where you can often see loons, rises Jo-Mary Mountain.

3.5 The trail climbs a low, rocky ridge beyond Henderson Pond. Long Pond is to your south, unseen down the steep slope. There is no access to Long Pond on this hike. Past Long Pond, the trail drops down the edge of jumbled cliffs and then along their bottom to intersect the Rabbit Pond Cutoff. This short trail skirts the east edge of Hedgehog Pond and ends at the Turtle Ridge Trail. (**Option:** You can use this trail to shorten the hike to 5.0 miles, but you would miss Turtle Ridge and Sing Sing Pond.) To continue the hike, turn left onto the Sing Sing Pond Trail.

3.9 The Sing Sing Pond Trail passes a small, marshy pond that has an unmarked trail to a large boulder at its edge.

4.6 The Sing Sing Pond Trail follows a stream, then comes out onto an old woods road. The trail skirts the east side of Sing Sing Pond, visible through the trees. Access to Sing Sing Pond is from the Turtle Ridge Trail. This section tends to be very buggy but offers the possibility of a moose sighting. The Sing Sing Pond Trail continues 1.0 mile to the Turtle Ridge west trailhead; turn right onto the Turtle Ridge Trail.

5.0 After crossing the outlet stream of Sing Sing Pond, the trail winds among large boulders and comes close to Sing Sing Pond. A short unmarked trail leads out to the pond, where there are boulders at its edge. This is a good spot to rest, swim, and watch for loons and moose. There are fine views across the pond of the three humps of Turtle Ridge.

5.8 Climb steadily to a junction with the Great Circle Trail. Continue straight on the Turtle Ridge Trail.

6.1 The Turtle Ridge Trail climbs up the west end of Turtle Ridge. The first summit hump is wooded, with only limited views. The second hump is open, and the trail passes across a high cliff top with views across Sing Sing Pond to White Cap and other mountains to the south.

6.3 The trail turns north from the cliffs and crosses the ridge. From the back of the ridge, there are limited views north of Katahdin. The trail then emerges onto the open summit of the third hump of Turtle Ridge, with unrestricted views in every direction except north.

7.0 The trail descends off Turtle Ridge and skirts below some cliffs then crosses through the woods to Hedgehog Pond. Where the Turtle Ridge Trail makes a left turn, a short, unmarked side trail leads to the pond.

7.1 Junction with the Rabbit Pond Cutoff. Continue straight on the Turtle Ridge Trail toward Rabbit Pond to complete the hike.

8.1 The Turtle Ridge Trail crosses a spine of granite then comes to Rabbit Pond. The trail crosses exposed granite bedrock at the east end of Rabbit Pond. The pond's outlet stream flows over the rock and disappears into the woods. The trail continues across the granite, climbing to the junction with the Henderson Pond Trail. This is a good area for finding blueberries. To return to the trailhead, turn left and descend off the exposed rock.

8.6 Arrive back at the trailhead.

18 Potaywadjo Ridge

Potaywadjo Ridge rises above the west end of Lower Jo-Mary Lake. A side trail off the Appalachian Trail climbs the rocky ridge to open ledges with wonderful views of Jo-Mary and the many lakes of the West Branch Penobscot River. The trail is a long way from anywhere and is little used, adding remoteness and solitude to the views.

Start: Bridge over Cooper Brook
Elevation gain: 1,087 feet
Distance: 8.2 miles out and back
Hiking time: About 5 hours
Difficulty: Moderate
Season: June–Oct
Trail surface: Woodland path
Land status: Appalachian Trail
Nearest town: Brownville
Other users: Hunters in season
Water availability: Cooper Brook
Canine compatibility: Dogs must be under control at all times.

Fees and permits: Access fee paid at Jo-Mary gatehouse
Maps: *DeLorme: Maine Atlas & Gazetteer:* Map 42; USGS Nahmakanta Stream
Trail contact: Nahmakanta Public Reserved Land; (207) 941-4412; maine.gov/nahmakanta
   KI Jo-Mary Forest; (207) 435-6213; northmainewoods.org
Amenities available: None
Maximum grade: 17% grade for 0.7 mile on the Potaywadjo Ridge Trail
Cell service: None

Finding the trailhead: From the bridge over the Pleasant River in Brownville on ME 11, drive north 15.7 miles. Turn left onto Jo-Mary Road at the Jo-Mary Campground sign. The gate where you pay the fee is 0.1 mile from ME 11. From the gate, drive 5.9 miles to a fork in the road. Turn right, staying on Jo-Mary Road. Drive 2.8 miles and turn right onto a smaller road at the sign for Buckhorn Camps. Drive 1.7 on the windy road through cut-over areas past several small side roads. Cross Duck Brook then almost immediately bear left at an intersection, staying on the main road. Drive another 2.4 miles on the same windy road. As you near Middle Jo-Mary Lake, a snowmobile trail goes off to the right and the road bears left. Almost immediately, you pass the road down to the boat launch (visible 100 feet away). The road passes through the Buckhorn Camps parking area, bears right, then almost immediately turns left. Drive 2.1 miles to the bridge over Cooper Brook. This last 2 miles is kinda rough. Just before the bridge there's a wide spot where you can carefully turn around. To start the hike, cross the bridge on foot and turn right onto the Appalachian Trail. Trailhead GPS: N45° 39.586' / W68° 59.555' (*Note:* If you're uncomfortable driving down the snowmobile trail, you can park in a gravelly area the road passes through about 1.5 miles from Buckhorn Camps.)

The Hike

If you're familiar with the Appalachian Trail in Maine, you've probably heard of Potaywadjo Spring, one of the largest in Maine. Water bubbles up out of a gravel bowl 10 feet across. Nearby is the swankiest lean-to in the state. It's maintained by

Lower Jo-Mary Lake from the ridge

L.L.Bean, and they spare no expense. The privy is a two-holer, with separate doors and curtains on the windows. Next to the lean-to is neatly stacked split firewood. Needless to say, thru-hikers talk about it a lot. What most hikers don't know is the trail to the top of nearby Potaywadjo Ridge. The trail is well blazed but faint in places because so few people use it.

Day hikers generally don't hike in this area either. It's a long hike from anywhere. If you hike in from where the Jo-Mary Road crosses the AT, you'd be looking at more than 13 miles in and out. I decided to find a shorter way.

I dug out all my maps and guides and realized that the AT crosses a snowmobile trail where the trail follows Cooper Brook. If I could get near Cooper Brook, I could cross and pick up the AT. Turns out, the snowmobile trail is drivable right up to the bridge over Cooper Brook, which is intact. That means I cut the 13-mile hike down to 8.2 miles out and back. That's manageable, and I didn't have to ford the stream.

From Cooper Brook, it's a short, easy hike to Mud Brook. You need to ford both channels just below Mud Pond. It's usually possible to cross without getting your feet wet—the first channel upstream from the trail; downstream on the second. After fording Mud Brook, the trail crosses a dry, pine-covered ridge with nice views of Mud

Gravelly beach on Lower Jo-Mary Lake

Pond. The trail turns away from Mud Pond and heads through classic Maine AT to Lower Jo-Mary Lake. This section is all rocks and roots held together by mud. But the woods are cool and beautiful. You come to a fork in the trail. The AT bears left, away from Lower Jo-Mary Lake. A blue-blazed trail bears right along the shore. Follow the blue-blazed trail into Antlers Campground. You come to a wide-open area in a stand of tall red pines. To your right is a small beach on the lake. Straight ahead is a trail that leads to several tent campsites. Turn left and walk away from the lake. In a short distance, you reach the AT. Turn right.

The trail leaves the shore of the lake and passes through mixed forest, much more open and sunny than the hike so far. Eventually the trail returns to the shore of Lower Jo-Mary Lake and crosses a gravel beach. The trail follows the curve of the shore, crossing a brook on rocks. You climb a bit away from the lake and reach the Potaywadjo Ridge Trail. A small sign facing the other way marks the trail. The trail itself is barely visible; it's pretty overgrown here. Turn left onto the Potaywadjo Ridge Trail.

Potaywadjo Ridge Trail is little hiked, so the trail bed is pretty faint in most places; however, the blue-blazed route is obvious. The climb begins gently through mostly hardwoods. As it steepens, the forest becomes more mixed. You climb up through a

Mud Pond Outlet

couple of boulder fields before reaching the first of the ledges. Parts of this climb are very steep, often with loose dirt covered with acorns. Luckily the trail doesn't go straight up the ridge; mostly you climb as you slab to the west.

Up on the ridge, the trail crosses three ledges separated by stands of twisted pines. Each successive ledge is more open, with wider views. Near the west end of the third ledge, instead of a blaze, the word "END" is painted on the rock. From here you have a fine view of the many lakes along the West Branch Penobscot River.

You can explore the ridge by following a series of interconnected ledges that trend north from the trail. However, none offers a view. Still, walking across the flat ledges surrounded by dense forest edged with berry bushes is a fine way to spend an afternoon.

Miles and Directions

0.0   Start by walking across the bridge over Cooper Brook; turn right onto the northbound AT.

0.5   Ford the two channels of Mud Brook just below the pond.

1.9   Loop around the east side of Mud Pond and then through rocky woods to the shore of Lower Jo-Mary Lake. Go straight onto a blue-blazed trail.

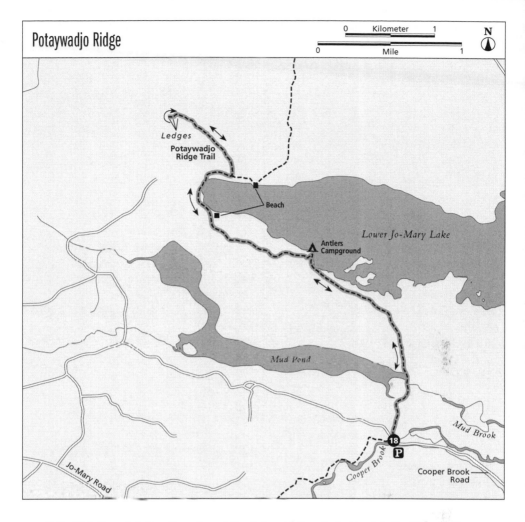

2.0 Walk through Antlers Campground. Turn left and follow the trail back to the AT. Turn right, back onto the northbound AT.

3.1 The trail leaves the lakeshore for a while, then comes back to it and crosses a gravelly beach.

3.4 The trail loops around the end of the lake, crossing a brook on rocks, then climbs to the Potaywadjo Ridge Trail. There's a small sign that faces the other way for the indistinct trail. If you reach a marked side trail to a beach, you've gone about 0.2 mile too far.

4.0 The well-blazed but indistinct trail climbs through the woods, then slabs up rocks to the first ledges.

4.1 The trail crosses three distinct ledges, each with a more-expansive view than the previous one. The trail ends where "END" is painted on the ledge in blue letters. To complete the hike, retrace your steps to the trailhead.

8.2 Arrive back at the trailhead.

19 Little Boardman Mountain

There are no views from the wooded summit of Little Boardman Mountain. On the approach you pass ledges with partial views south and north. The climb is fairly easy and passes through pretty woods with lots of wildflowers. A short distance northbound on the Appalachian Trail from the trailhead is a sand beach on the south end of Crawford Pond.

Start: Southbound AT at the Johnston Pond Road crossing
Elevation gain: 796 feet
Distance: 2.8 miles out and back
Hiking time: About 3 hours
Difficulty: Easy
Season: June–Oct
Trail surface: Woodland path
Land status: Appalachian Trail
Nearest town: Brownville
Other users: None
Water availability: None
Canine compatibility: Dogs must be under control at all times.

Fees and permits: Access fee paid at the Jo-Mary gatehouse
Maps: *DeLorme: Maine Atlas & Gazetteer:* Map 42; USGS Big Shanty Mountain
Trail contact: North Maine Woods, Inc.; (207) 435-6213; northmainewoods.org
Amenities available: Sand beach near trailhead
Maximum grade: Fairly consistent 10% grade for 1.3 miles on climb to Little Boardman Mountain
Cell service: None

Finding the trailhead: From the bridge over the Pleasant River in Brownville on ME 11, drive north 15.7 miles. Turn left onto Jo-Mary Road at the Jo-Mary Campground sign. The gate where you pay the fee is 0.1 mile from ME 11. From the gate, drive 5.9 miles to a fork in the road. Go straight onto Johnson Pond Road and drive 4.5 miles. Pass Johnston Pond. Continue 2.6 miles and bear left at the intersection. Drive 0.5 mile and bear right at the intersection. Drive 1.1 miles and park on the shoulder where the AT crosses the road. The trailhead is the southbound AT, on the left. Trailhead GPS: N45° 37.000' / W69° 07.845'

The Hike

When you hike north on the AT from White Cap, the trail descends and crosses the wide valley of East Branch Pleasant River. The trail heads to the Jo-Mary Lakes, then loops to the west to Nahmakanta Lake before climbing Nesuntabunt Mountain. This long, low stretch is what gives the 100 Mile Wilderness its reputation among thru-hikers as being flat. The only mountain in the entire section is Little Boardman. There's no view from the top, so most people don't take much notice of this little gem.

It's a fun and easy hike that does have some views. And after the hike you can visit a nearby sand beach for an afternoon swim. The hike begins where Johnston Pond

View of Katahdin

Road crosses the AT in deep woods. You climb gently through dappled light, the woods full of rocks and wildflowers. The trail turns south and climbs more steadily for a short time. You pass beneath a mossy cliff then climb to its shoulder. Where the trail turns left, turn right and bushwhack 100 feet to the edge of the cliff. Between the trees, you have a fine view of Katahdin.

Past this cliff, the trail is often on bare bedrock. One large ledge offers a partial view to the south. A short, easy climb past the ledges brings you to the summit—a grove of widely spaced evergreens that teases you with the possibility of an overlook that doesn't exist. If you were to continue southbound on the AT, the trail drops quickly off Little Boardman Mountain to East Branch Pleasant River. There are some partial views of White Cap along the way.

When you make it back to your car parked along Johnston Pond Road, continue northbound on the AT. In 0.1 mile the trail crosses a wide gravel streambed. Turn left on this (it's actually a side trail) and walk 0.1 mile to the south shore of Crawford Pond. You'll emerge onto a long arc of pale sand. It's a great beach. You can see across the large pond to beaches on the north and west shores, where there are campsites.

Little Boardman Mountain

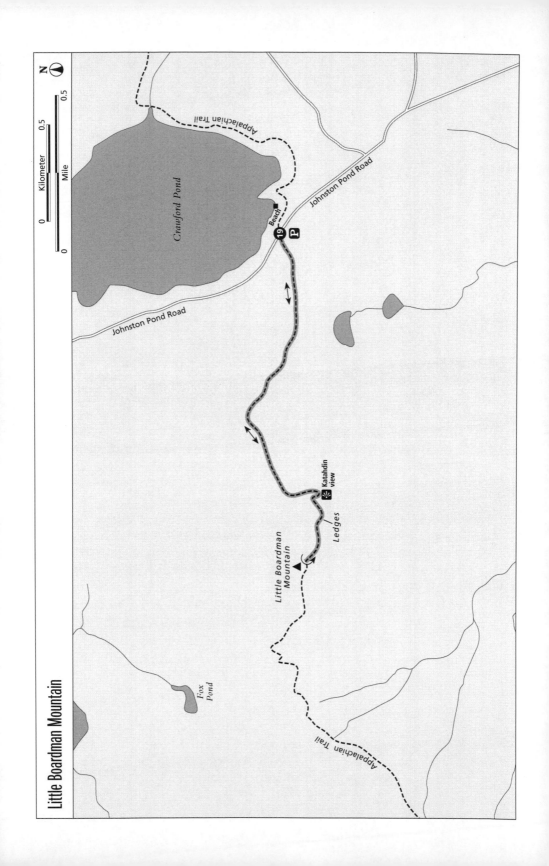

The open ledges near the summit

Miles and Directions

0.0 Start on the southbound AT.

1.1 Climb gently. After a short steep climb, you can bushwhack 100 feet off-trail to the right to get a view of Katahdin.

1.2 Reach open ledges with a partial view south.

1.4 A marked side trail leads 100 feet to the wooded summit. To complete the hike, retrace your steps to the trailhead.

2.8 Arrive back at the trailhead. (**Option:** Cross the road and continue northbound on the AT for 0.1 mile. Turn left onto a side trail that looks like a gravel streambed. This trail leads in 0.1 mile to a sand beach on Crawford Pond.)

20 Gauntlet Falls

The East Branch Pleasant River drops 15 feet into a narrow slot between two huge slabs of bedrock. Below the falls is a large, deep pool. The streambed and shore are littered with huge blocks of black stone for the next 1,000 yards. In the middle of this jumble of rock is a 10-foot slide waterfall with a deep pool at its base. Farther downstream are a series of stair falls before Mud Gauntlet Brook. Mud Gauntlet Falls is almost 0.5 mile up this untrailed stream.

Start: Gauntlet Falls Trailhead
Elevation gain: 362 feet
Distance: 2.0 miles out and back
Hiking time: About 2 hours
Difficulty: Moderate; most of the hike is a bushwhack
Season: Late May–Oct (*Note:* Avoid on weekends, when Gauntlet Falls is often an overcrowded camping and party site.)
Trail surface: Slate bedrock, rocky shore
Land status: KI Jo-Mary Forest
Nearest town: Brownville
Other users: Anglers and hunters in season
Water availability: None

Canine compatibility: Dogs must be under control at all times.
Fees and permits: Access fee paid at Jo-Mary gatehouse
Maps: *DeLorme: Maine Atlas & Gazetteer:* Map 42; USGS Jo-Mary Mountain
Trail contact: North Maine Woods, Inc.; (207) 435-6213; northmainewoods.org
Amenities available: Outhouse at the trailhead
Maximum grade: This hike has almost no grade; the climbing is going up and down boulders and slabs along the stream.
Cell service: None

Finding the trailhead: From the bridge over the Pleasant River in Brownville on ME 11, drive north 15.7 miles. Turn left onto Jo-Mary Road at the Jo-Mary Campground sign. The gate where you pay the fee is 0.1 mile from ME 11. From the gate, drive 6 miles to a fork in the road. Go straight at the fork onto Johnson Pond Road and drive 2.7 miles. Turn left onto B Pond Road at the large snowplow. Drive 1.3 miles, passing Jo-Mary Pond. Turn left onto Gauntlet Falls Road and continue 1.5 miles. Bear right at the fork (East Branch campsite 2 is to the hard right) and drive 0.1 mile to the day-use parking area at the end of the road. The trailhead is on the south side of the parking area, next to campsite 1. Trailhead GPS: N45° 32.463' / W69° 02.198'

The Hike

The West Branch Pleasant River has Gulf Hagas. The East Branch has Gauntlet Falls. Both features are defined by black slate. At Gauntlet Falls, the river drops 15 feet into a crack between two huge blocks of slate. On the far shore, the bedrock is a jumble of angles and weathered slabs that nearly block the river. On the near side, the slate rises smooth and straight 20 feet above the river. You can stand atop this formation and look straight down at Gauntlet Falls. The bedrock angles down next to the river at a manageable 30 degrees. Below the falls is a deep, dark pool. The water is full of tannin picked up from spruce roots. The pool is at least 20 feet deep in the middle.

Gauntlet Falls from the gravel island

Below the pool, the river goes around a gravel island. The best view of the waterfall is from the head of the island. By late June you can easily cross to the island without getting your feet wet. But why? This is a great swimming spot—deep, cool water and lots of flat, smooth slate to relax on. Unfortunately, many people have written their names on the bedrock, dating back to 1881. This spot tends to be crowded on weekends.

To continue the hike and get more solitude, bushwhack down the shore on the east side. You can walk in the shallows along the shore or scramble over and around the boulders. At 0.1 mile downstream, you'll come to a large bedrock eruption that crosses the river. A slot in it allows the river to slide down the sculpted rock, dropping 10 feet into a very deep pool. This is Lower Gauntlet Falls.

Continue downstream another 0.4 mile. Mud Gauntlet Brook flows into the river from the west. To get there, you clamber over the ruggedest part of the river. Giant slabs of slate like black panes of glass litter the shore. Ledges jut into the river and even across it. The river drops through a series of pretty stair falls. To get past this section, you have to get wet, hike up in the woods to get around the high boulders and slabs, or do a lot of rock scrambling.

Mud Gauntlet Falls

The last waterfall before the ford of the river

Cross the river on stones below the last waterfall—you can see the river flatten out below you and bend east—and above a good-size pool. Bushwhack up and over a rocky hill to Mud Gauntlet Brook, just upstream from the river. You can follow either the stream in its bed or through the woods. Some combination of the two is easiest. In 0.4 mile you'll reach the base of Mud Gauntlet Falls. It's really several waterfalls, hemmed in by bedrock. The largest drop is a horsetail down a joint fracture in the rock. The total drop is about 30 feet. Note that along East Branch Pleasant River, all the rock was black slate. Here the bedrock is gray and much rougher.

Miles and Directions

0.0 Start at the Gauntlet Falls Trailhead, at the west side of the parking area. In 100 feet you reach the top of Gauntlet Falls. Climb the bedrock to your left.

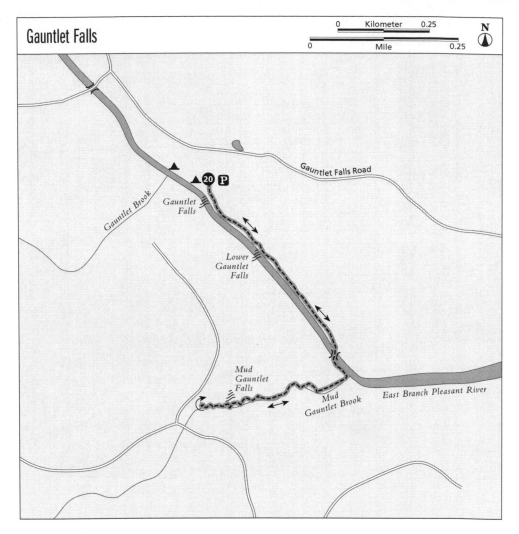

Gauntlet Falls

0.1 Stand atop the slate, looking straight down at the falls. Descend the slate to the river below the falls. After exploring the island and pool, follow the river downstream. Mostly you can stay beside the river without getting your feet wet.

0.2 Reach Lower Gauntlet Falls. Here the best option is to hike into the woods around the high ledges and return to the river at the pool below the falls. There is a short trail here.

0.5 Pass a series of stair falls hemmed in by huge boulders and bedrock slabs. Use your judgment to decide when to stay beside the river and when to hike into the woods to get around high rocks. Cross the river on stones below the last waterfall.

0.6 Reach Mud Gauntlet Brook, flowing in from the west. Bushwhack upstream on the right side of the brook.

1.0 Reach the base of Mud Gauntlet Falls. To complete the hike, retrace your steps to the trailhead.

2.0 Arrive back at the trailhead.

21 White Cap Mountain via Logan Brook

This is the more popular route up White Cap Mountain. You follow Logan Brook and leave it at the lean-to and waterfall. There's a spectacular overlook along the trail before reaching tree line. Above tree line you have amazing views in every direction. You can see from the Bigelows to Katahdin and beyond.

Start: Gate across Frenchtown Road
Elevation gain: 2,193 feet
Distance: 6.6 miles out and back
Hiking time: About 5 hours
Difficulty: Strenuous
Season: June–Oct
Trail surface: Woodland path
Land status: Appalachian Trail
Nearest town: Greenville
Other users: None
Water availability: Logan Brook
Canine compatibility: Dogs must be under control at all times.

Fees and permits: No fees or permits required
Maps: *DeLorme: Maine Atlas & Gazetteer:* Maps 41 and 42; USGS Big Shanty Mountain
Trail contact: None
Amenities available: None
Maximum grade: Average 10% grade from trailhead to summit. Three sections average more than 30%: a short climb as soon as you get on the AT, just past the lean-to, and between the overlook and tree line.
Cell service: Spotty service on the summit

Finding the trailhead: From the blinking light in Greenville, drive north on Lily Bay Road for 17.7 miles. Just before reaching Kokadjo and Roach River, turn right onto Frenchtown Road. Drive 13.8 miles, staying straight on Frenchtown Road the whole time. There's one section between two bridges where the road passes between the West Branch Ponds. The road here is narrower and rougher. Otherwise, the road is wide and well-maintained. Park on the shoulder just before the gate across the road. The trailhead is at the gate. Trailhead GPS: N45° 34.600' / W69° 13.818'

The Hike

White Cap Mountain is the highest point in the 100 Mile Wilderness and the highest mountain on the Appalachian Trail between the Bigelows and Katahdin. You can see those mountains from the summit. The mountain is the anchor of a range running east–west from Gulf Hagas Mountain to White Cap. Southeast of White Cap are a group of untrailed 3,000-footers. As a result, the summit offers wild and spectacular views in every direction.

The first 0.5 mile of the hike follows a logging road, then you turn right onto the southbound AT. Climb steadily up a shoulder and pick up Logan Brook. You follow the brook, climbing gently to the Logan Brook Lean-to. There's a small but pretty waterfall on the brook next to the lean-to.

Looking west from just before the summit to Big and Little Spencer Mountains

The trail climbs steadily away from the brook to the spine of a ridge. The trail turns right and climbs the ridge. You pass a very short side trail to a rocky overlook perched on the rim of the ridge. The valley below you appears to be a cirque with almost vertical sides. You can hear but not see Logan Brook crashing down the face.

The trail climbs steadily, mostly on stone steps, to tree line. As you emerge from the forest onto the broken rocks around the wooded summit, Big and Little Spencer Mountains are to your right; Katahdin is behind you. As you near the summit, the nearby mountains to the south become visible: Big and Little Spruce and Big and Little Shanty. Three of the four are also over 3,000 feet elevation. The south face of White Cap just below the summit is a large expanse of open loose rocks. This large area of rock is visible from Bangor and gives the mountain its name. The actual summit is within an area of dwarf spruce surrounded by bare rock.

To the south and southwest, you can see the other mountains in the White Cap Range, the Barren Range across the Pleasant River valley, and mountains to the horizon, where the Bigelows are visible.

Stairs on the climb to tree line

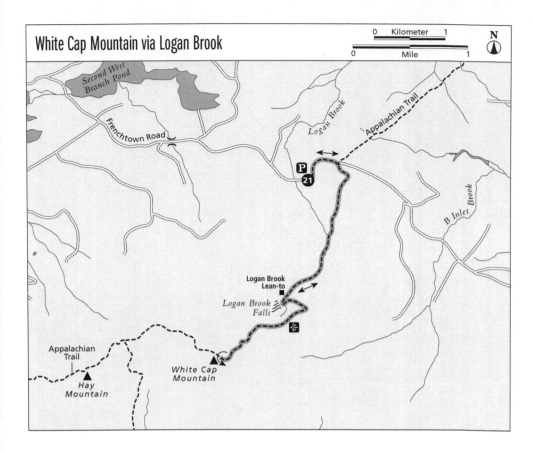

White Cap Mountain via Logan Brook

Miles and Directions

0.0 Start at the gate and follow Frenchtown Road east.

0.4 Turn right off the road onto the southbound AT.

1.2 Climb steadily to Logan Brook.

2.0 Climb gently beside Logan Brook to the Logan Brook Lean-to. One hundred feet beyond the lean-to is a waterfall on Logan Brook. The AT turns left at the lean-to.

2.5 Climb steadily onto the ridge and then up the ridge to an overlook.

3.0 Climb steadily and break out of the trees.

3.3 The AT loops east around and then to the summit of White Cap Mountain. To complete the hike, retrace your steps to the trailhead.

6.6 Arrive back at the trailhead.

22 White Cap Mountain via White Brook

This hike follows the old fire warden's trail to the saddle between Hay and White Cap Mountains. This climb is a little easier than climbing White Cap from Frenchtown Road. White Cap's open summit offers spectacular views in every direction. You can see everything from the Bigelows to Katahdin and the untrailed 3,000-footers next door.

Start: Gravel pit at end of High Bridge Road
Elevation gain: 1,838 feet
Distance: 6.4 miles out and back
Hiking time: About 5 hours
Difficulty: Moderate
Season: June–Oct
Trail surface: Woodland path
Land status: Appalachian Trail corridor
Nearest town: Brownville
Other users: Hunters on lower section of the hike in season
Water availability: White Brook
Canine compatibility: Dogs must be under control at all times.
Fees and permits: Access fee paid at Katahdin Iron Works gate

Maps: *DeLorme: Maine Atlas & Gazetteer:* Map 42; USGS Hay Mountain and Big Shanty Mountain
Trail contact: Maine Appalachian Trail Club; matc.org
KI Jo-Mary Forest; (207) 435-6213; northmainewoods.org
Amenities available: Swimming hole at High Bridge on the drive in
Maximum grade: Average 9.8% from trailhead to summit. Two sections average greater than 30%: the climb above the waterfall on White Brook and the climb from turning right onto the AT to tree line.
Cell service: Spotty reception on the summit

Finding the trailhead: Drive north 4.9 miles from the bridge over the Pleasant River in Brownville. Turn left onto the KI Road at the sign for Gulf Hagas and drive 6.5 miles to Katahdin Iron Works. Register and pay an entrance fee here. Cross the West Branch Pleasant River, turn right, and drive 3.5 miles. Bear right at the sign for High Bridge and drive 2.2 miles. Turn left, cross High Bridge, and continue another 3.7 miles. This section of road has several spots that are either washed out or very rough. The worst is about 2 miles beyond High Bridge. I made it in my Honda CRV, but it's pretty sketchy. The road ends at a large gravel cul-de-sac with a huge pile of gravel at the far end. Park here. The trailhead is the continuation of the road next to the gravel pile. Trailhead GPS: N45° 31.919' / W69° 16.111'

The Hike

On your drive to the trailhead, you cross High Bridge then pass the interesting gorge above it. Be sure to stop and check out this interesting feature and its waterfalls. There are two campsites at the bridge. The road above High Bridge was impassable for years, but new logging has opened the area up again. Still, this road has a couple of seriously rough patches.

Looking west from the summit

The hike begins where the road ends at a huge pile of gravel. There's no trail sign or blazes, but the route is obvious. The first mile follows an old roadbed, although it's so old that in many places it feels more like a moose trail. This is a good place to find moose, which like to eat the young hardwoods along the trail. You get occasional views of White Cap Mountain along this section. Eventually the hike comes to a round meadow that used to be the turnaround at the end of the road. A cairn to the left marks the beginning of the old fire warden's trail.

From here the trail is well marked and maintained. In 2020 the upper section was rerouted and made easier by the MATC volunteer who maintained this section. You climb gently to White Brook, crossing the brook at a small waterfall. Above the falls, you climb more steadily. You pass a signed junction in the woods where there's no junction; this is where the fire warden's cabin used to be. There used to be a very

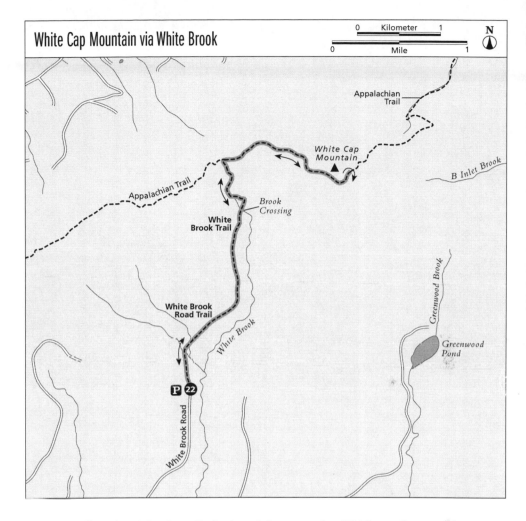

White Cap Mountain via White Brook

steep trail to the right that climbed straight up to the AT. The trail now slabs west before climbing.

The climb is pretty, with lots of mossy boulders and irregular ledges. The White Brook Trail ends at the AT in the saddle between Hay and White Cap Mountains. Turn right and climb steadily. Where you emerge from the trees, look to the left and get a view of Katahdin. The trail levels out on the open rocks as you near the summit. Be sure to follow the trail around the summit to the northeast side to get more views.

Miles and Directions

0.0 Start at the trailhead and follow the road around the large gravel pile.

1.2 This section of trail is easy to follow. Sometimes it's a trail, sometimes an old road, and sometimes it seems like a moose trail. There are occasional blazes and cairns. The trail

Katahdin from the north side of the summit

comes to an open, grassy area. Stay to the left and look for a cairn. The White Brook Trail proper begins at the cairn.

1.6 Climb gently to a crossing of White Brook.

1.7 Climb steadily to a ju in the woods. The trail turns left here.

2.1 Climb steadily, switchbacking up to the AT. Turn right onto the AT.

3.2 Climb steadily. As you near the summit, you get views to the north of Katahdin. A short side trail leads north into the trees to the summit. To complete the hike, retrace your steps to the trailhead. (***Option:*** Continue 0.1 mile farther northbound on the AT for open views north and northwest.)

6.4 Arrive back at the trailhead.

23 Hay Brook Falls

Hay Brook Falls is a 30-foot double drop on a stream that flows into Pleasant River a few miles below Gulf Hagas. It's an easy walk to this little-visited gem.

Start: Gulf Hagas Trailhead
Elevation gain: 254 feet
Distance: 2.6 miles out and back
Hiking time: About 2 hours
Difficulty: Easy
Season: Late May–Oct
Trail surface: Woodland path
Land status: KI Jo-Mary Forest
Nearest town: Brownville
Other users: None
Water availability: Pleasant River and Hay Brook

Canine compatibility: Dogs must be under control at all times.
Fees and permits: Access fee paid at Katahdin Iron Works gate
Maps: *DeLorme: Maine Atlas & Gazetteer:* Map 42; USGS Barren Mountain East
Trail contact: North Maine Woods, Inc.; (207) 435-6213
Amenities available: None
Maximum grade: Very little climbing except the short climb from the base of the waterfall to its top
Cell service: None

Finding the trailhead: From the bridge over the Pleasant River in Brownville, follow ME 11 north for 4.8 miles. Turn left onto the KI Road at the sign for Katahdin Iron Works and Gulf Hagas. Drive 6.5 miles to the gate, where you pay your fee. Cross the Pleasant River and turn right; continue 3.5 miles to a fork in the road. Take the left fork, following the signs to Gulf Hagas, and drive 2.9 miles. The parking area is on the right, at the sign for Gulf Hagas. Trailhead GPS: N45° 28.667' / W69° 17.122'

The Hike

Most sources give directions to Hay Brook Falls via High Bridge and the three campsites along Hay Brook just below the falls. The problem is the road is impassible and has been closed. As a result, most people miss out on this gem of a waterfall. But there's another route to the falls: via Gulf Hagas Trailhead.

From the trailhead, ford Pleasant River. The river is 100 feet across and usually about shin deep. The streambed is composed of slippery, round rocks. It's best to bring water shoes for the crossing.

Across the river, follow the Appalachian Trail northbound as it loops around The Hermitage—a grove of old-growth white pines. Come to a T intersection. The AT turns left toward Gulf Hagas. The sign gives no indication what's to the right—Hay Brook Falls is. Turn right and follow a wide, flat trail along the river past a pond then several backcountry campsites.

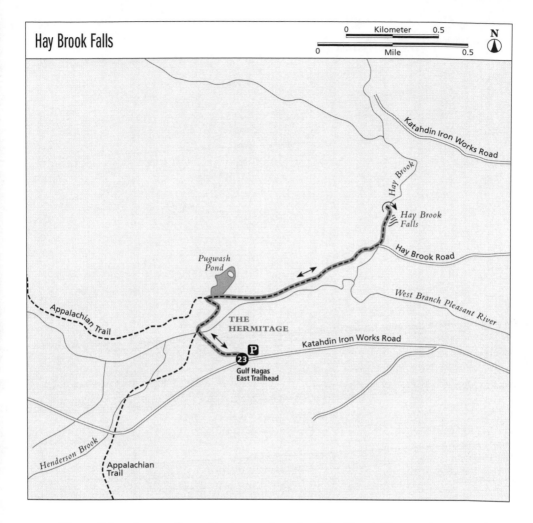

The trail bends away from the river and reaches Hay Brook. You need to cross the stream; either ford it or look for a spot just upstream, where you can cross on rocks. Across the stream, turn left and hike through three campsites. An unmarked but obvious trail leads upstream beyond the campsites. In no time, you can see Hay Brook Falls upstream. The trail passes several places where you can step out onto rocks along the stream for a view as the trail climbs to the top of the waterfall.

Hay Brook drops into a pool cupped in the cliff face, makes a turn, then drops 20 more feet into a good-size pool. The pool is surrounded by flat slate boulders, making this a great swimming hole. The rock face around the pool is smooth black slate that gets very mossy as it blends into the hillside.

Hay Brook Falls

Miles and Directions

0.0 Start at the Gulf Hagas Trailhead

0.2 Follow the Gulf Hagas Connector Trail to the Appalachian Trail and the Pleasant River. Ford the river.

0.4 Follow the AT northbound to a T intersection. Turn right off the AT.

0.6 Pass Pugwash Pond and Pleasant River campsite 10.

1.1 Pass campsites 7–9. Reach Hay Brook and cross the stream. Turn left and pass through Hay Brook campsites 1–3.

1.2 Follow an obvious but unmarked trail from campsite 3 upstream to an overlook of Hay Brook Falls.

1.3 The trail continues past the base of the falls to the top of the falls. To complete your hike, retrace your steps to the trailhead.

2.6 Arrive back at the trailhead.

24 Number Four Mountain

The trail up Number Four Mountain switchbacks up the steep-sided mountain, with occasional views north of Big and Little Spencer Mountains. The trail levels out and crosses the summit ridge through abundant wildflowers to the fire tower. You can climb the tower for a view or continue another 0.1 mile to an open overlook with spectacular views east, south, and west.

Start: Number Four Mountain Trailhead, on the east side of Meadow Brook Road
Distance: 3.8 miles out and back
Elevation gain: 1,502 feet
Hiking time: About 3 hours
Difficulty: Most challenging
Season: Best May–Oct
Trail surface: Woodland path
Land status: Private timber lands
Nearest town: Greenville
Other users: Hunters in season

Water availability: None
Canine compatibility: Dogs must be under control at all times.
Fees and permits: No fees or permits required
Maps: *DeLorme: Maine Atlas & Gazetteer:* Map 41; USGS Number Four Mountain
Trail contact: None
Amenities available: None
Maximum grade: Climb from the brook to the summit ridge averages 20.5% grade for 1.2 miles.
Cell service: On summit ridge

Finding the trailhead: From the blinking light in Greenville, drive north on Lily Bay Road for 13.1 miles. Turn right onto Meadow Brook Road at the sign for the hike and drive 1.7 miles. Turn left, staying on Meadow Brook Road, and continue 2.4 miles. The trailhead is on the right. Parking is another 0.1 mile ahead, also on the right. Trailhead GPS: N45° 37.912' / W69° 25.124'

The Hike

In 2015 the state finished rebuilding the trail up Number Four Mountain. Bog boards were added to the wet first section. Where a long line of bog boards skirt the boggy edges of Lagoon Brook, look for jack-in-the-pulpits carpeting the forest floor. This is the largest patch of these unique wildflowers I've found in Maine.

The trail climbs away from the brook through a regenerating area of bushy maples and moose trails. The forest transitions to larger evergreens as the trail steepens. Like all fire warden trails, this one used to go straight up the steep mountainside. The biggest change the state made to the trail was on this section, adding numerous switchbacks, which will cut down on erosion and make the climb more manageable. About 0.5 mile was added to the hike.

The trail reaches the north end of the summit ridge and becomes more gentle. The hike across the ridge to the tower on the summit passes through abundant wildflowers in season. You can climb the fire tower to get a 360-degree view. Or, if you don't trust old fire towers—in this case, one whose cabin lies broken in the woods nearby—continue on the trail another 0.1 mile to two overlooks.

The overlook

Moosehead Lake and Lily Bay Mountain from the overlook

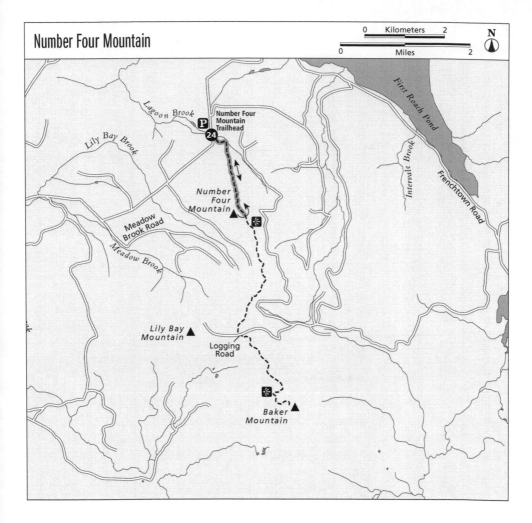

The view east, south, and west from the overlooks is spectacular. Baker and Lily Bay Mountains lie just to the south. Around them to the southwest and west is Moosehead Lake. There's a bench at the overlook where you can sit and enjoy the mountain and lakes around you.

Miles and Directions

0.0 Start from the trailhead on the east side of Meadow Brook Road.

0.3 The trail turns south away from Lagoon Brook and begins to climb.

1.8 The trail switchbacks up the steep mountainside to the summit. Continue over the summit past the tower.

1.9 The trail reaches two overlooks with fine views in all directions except north. To complete the hike, return the way you came.

3.8 Arrive back at the trailhead.

25 Baker Mountain

This hike crosses Number Four Mountain, with its spectacular view across Moosehead Lake and of the Lily Bay Mountains. The trail descends off Number Four and crosses a long ridge to Baker Mountain. As you climb you have partial views east to Katahdin, north past Number Four Mountain, and west to Moosehead Lake. The trail ends on Baker Mountain's wooded summit.

Start: Number Four Mountain Trailhead
Elevation gain: 3,587 feet
Distance: 12.2 miles out and back
Hiking time: About 8 hours
Difficulty: Strenuous; after all, you're climbing two mountains.
Season: June–Oct
Trail surface: Woodland path
Land status: Private timberlands and AMC preserve
Nearest town: Greenville
Other users: Hunters in season
Water availability: None

Canine compatibility: Dogs must be under control at all times.
Fees and permits: No fees or permits required
Other maps: *DeLorme: Maine Atlas & Gazetteer:* Map 41; USGS Number Four Mountain
Trail contact: None
Amenities available: None
Maximum grade: Climb from the brook to Number Four Mountain's summit ridge averages 20.5% grade for 1.2 miles. The last mile to Baker Mountain's summit averages 10% grade, with short climbs as steep as 40% grade.
Cell service: Spotty reception throughout the hike

Finding the trailhead: From the blinking light in Greenville, drive north on Lily Bay Road for 13.1 miles. Turn right onto Meadow Brook Road at the sign for the hike and drive 1.7 miles. Turn left, staying on Meadow Brook Road, and continue 2.4 miles. The trailhead is on the right. Parking is another 0.1 mile ahead, also on the right. Trailhead GPS: N45° 37.912' / W69° 25.124'

The Hike

The first 2 miles of this hike follow the Number Four Mountain Trail. Past the summit overlook, descend Number Four Mountain. This section is pretty steep, with some views. Once off the mountain, the trail roller-coasters along. You pass through various types of forest—some with lots of ferns, others more mossy or wet—or small meadows of wildflowers. Even several years after an Appalachian Mountain Club (AMC) crew built this trail, it still feels new. The trail reaches a snowmobile trail and turns left onto it. In a short distance, turn right off the snowmobile trail and begin climbing.

The trail crosses a ledgy knob with a semi-open summit. This knob is part of Baker Mountain's complex and large massif. After descending off the knob, you begin climbing in earnest. The trail climbs through semi-open hardwoods with views east and north. You can see Katahdin through the trees on the steepest section. The trail

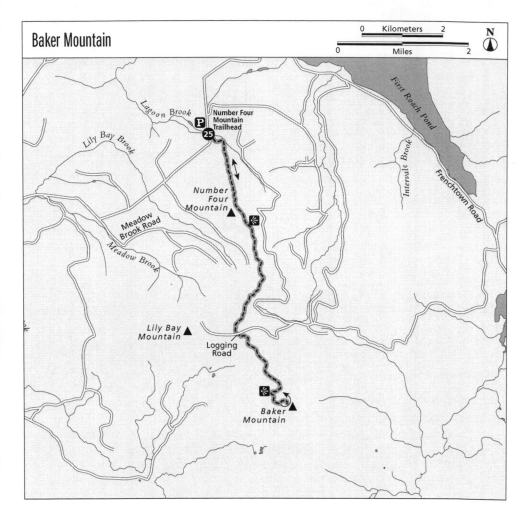

climbs out of the hardwoods and into evergreens, mostly undersized spruce. The stunted spruce trees allow for nice views west as you near the summit.

Baker Mountain's summit is wooded. For now the trail ends at the register. AMC has long planned to continue the trail over the mountain and descend to Horseshoe Pond. We can all look forward to that. There will be open ledges with views along that trail. For now, enjoy the views of Moosehead Lake and the other Lily Bay Mountains from near the summit. And keep your eyes peeled for Katahdin on your descent.

Looking back toward Number Four Mountain

Miles and Directions

0.0 Start from the trailhead on the east side of Meadow Brook Road.

0.3 The trail turns south, away from Lagoon Brook, and begins to climb.

1.8 The trail switchbacks up the steep mountainside to the summit. Continue over the summit past the tower.

1.9 The trail reaches two overlooks with fine views in all directions except north.

4.1 Descend steadily off Number Four Mountain, then roller-coaster along a series of wooded ridges. Turn left onto an old logging road used as a snowmobile trail; then turn right, back onto the hiking trail.

5.5 Climb steadily over a series of humps to a steep section with a view of Katahdin.

6.1 Climb steadily. As you near the summit, the stunted spruce trees allow for fine views. Reach the wooded summit. To complete the hike, retrace your steps to the trailhead.

12.2 Arrive back at the trailhead.

26 Indian Mountain

This is a short but very steep hike up Indian Mountain to Laurie's Ledge and an over-look just west of the mountain's summit. The two overlooks offer spectacular views of the surrounding mountains and ponds. The hike itself passes through beech forest and then climbs up into the spruce-and-rock forest atop the mountain, passing several geologically interesting features.

Start: Laurie's Ledge trailhead
Distance: 3.0 miles out and back
Elevation gain: 1,025 feet
Hiking time: 2-3 hours
Difficulty: Strenuous; the hike is short but climbs more than 1,000 feet.
Season: Best June-Oct
Trail surface: Woodland path
Land status: AMC North Woods Recreation and Conservation Area
Nearest town: Greenville
Other users: None
Water availability: None
Canine compatibility: Dogs must be under control at all times.

Fees and permits: Access fee paid at the Hedgehog gate on the KI Road
Maps: *DeLorme: Maine Atlas & Gazetteer:* Map 41; USGS Number Four Mountain and Hay Mountain.
Trail contact: Appalachian Mountain Club, Greenville Office; (207) 695-3085; outdoors.org
Amenities available: None
Maximum grade: Average 11% grade from trailhead to summit; short sections to and above the cliffs as steep as 35%
Cell service: Spotty reception from west overlook

Finding the trailhead: From the blinking light in Greenville, drive north on Lily Bay Road. Almost immediately turn right onto Pleasant Street. As you leave Greenville, the road becomes East Road. The pavement ends at the airport. At Lower Wilson Pond, the road becomes the KI Road. There are numerous side roads, which change from year to year depending on the needs of the logging companies. The Appalachian Mountain Club (AMC) has put up signs directing you to their lodges at most side roads. Follow the signs to their lodges, staying on the KI Road. At 12.1 miles from the blinking light in Greenville, you reach the Hedgehog checkpoint, where you need to pay the fee. Past the checkpoint, drive 2.9 miles. Turn left onto Little Lyford Ponds Road and drive 2.3 miles to the trailhead parking, on the left. Trailhead GPS: N45° 31.041' / W69° 21.933'

The Hike

The hike to Laurie's Ledge on Indian Mountain begins as a pleasant meander through a beech forest. The trail climbs around exposed bedrock, passing a view east of the Little Lyford Ponds and, across them, Gulf Hagas Mountain. Unseen on the south shore of the ponds is the Little Lyford Camps. Since being built in 1874, this commercial camp was popular with trout enthusiasts, who enjoyed the rustic cabins and isolated setting. In 2003 the Appalachian Mountain Club (AMC) bought the camps and 60,000 acres of land around them as part of their North Woods Initiative. They

View across Little Lyford Ponds from near the trailhead

have developed more than 80 miles of hiking and skiing trails on their lands that connect to the nearby Appalachian Trail and to Gulf Hagas. The Laurie's Ledge Trail is one of the most scenic.

The trail climbs to an old woods road that it shares with the ski trail that circles Indian Mountain to Horseshoe Pond. When the yellow-blazed Laurie's Ledge Trail leaves the ski trail, you begin to climb. The trail passes four very large moss and fern covered boulders that appear, at one time, to have been one huge piece of rock. The trail climbs more steeply to a cliff—perhaps the original home of the boulders below. Take time to study the cliff through the screen of trees. Note that the rock has cleaved along straight lines and almost forms a box canyon. The bedrock here is clearly not granite, which weathers and breaks apart very differently. The trail turns south and follows along the bottom of the cliff; it then turns west and climbs very steeply, with some views to the south. Across the wide valley rises Barren Mountain.

A short side trail, marked with a sign, leads out to a bench atop Laurie's Ledge. From the rocky vantage, you can see northeast to southeast. To the northeast are the Boardman Mountains and the wooded summits south of the Roach Ponds. Across Little Lyford Ponds is Gulf Hagas Mountain; behind it you can see the rest of the chain, ending with the bare summit of White Cap Mountain. Between those two views, and farther in the distance, is Katahdin.

Beyond Laurie's Ledge, the trail climbs very steeply up Indian Mountain, then slabs to the north around its summit without crossing it. The forest is dark and moss covered. Boulders lie in jumbles beneath the spruce. The trail ends at a rough opening just below the summit, with fine views to the west and north. Below is Horseshoe Pond, and across it rises the almost vertical east face of Elephant Mountain. One of two mountains in Maine with that name—the other is in the Rangeley Lakes region

Horseshoe Pond and Elephant Mountain from the west overlook

and crossed by the AT—it got its name because it looks like an elephant when viewed from this point. This Elephant Mountain is most famous for the remains of a B-52 bomber that lie on its flank after crashing in 1963. The only trail on the mountain leads to the wreckage, well short of the summit or any views. Beyond Elephant Mountain, you can see Big Moose Mountain and Moosehead Lake. To the north rises Baker Mountain, the highest of the Lily Bay Mountains.

Miles and Directions

0.0   Start at the Laurie's Ledge Trailhead, behind the parking area.

0.3   The yellow-blazed trail climbs gently through the woods with views of Little Lyford Pond and Gulf Hagas Mountain to a junction with the Indian Mountain Circuit ski trail. Turn right onto the wide trail. The two trails follow the same route for the next 0.3 mile.

0.6   The ski trail continues straight ahead; the hike follows the Laurie's Ledge Trail to the left.

0.7   The trail climbs gently, passing among a group of very large boulders.

0.8   The trail climbs more steeply to the foot of a cliff. The trail follows along the cliff then begins climbing in earnest.

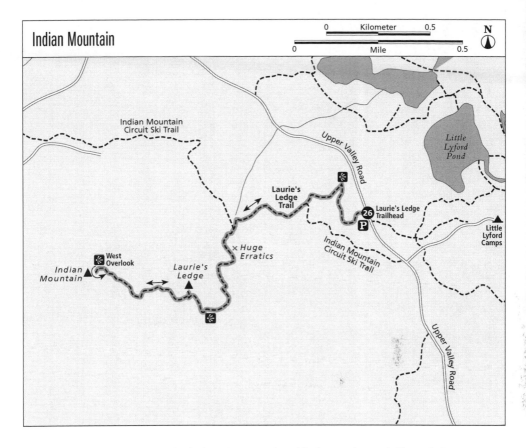

1.1 As the trail begins to climb, there is an opening with views to the south. The trail climbs steeply to a side trail that leads 100 feet to an overlook with a bench: Laurie's Ledge. From the overlook there are views east of the Gulf Hagas–Whitecap Mountain Range. When the air is especially clear, you can see Katahdin over the low mountains to the northeast.

1.5 Continue climbing past the overlook side trail. Almost immediately there is an opening with views to the south and west. The trail climbs, then slabs around the summit of Indian Mountain. The trail ends at a rough clearing just below the mountain's summit, with fine views west. You can see Elephant Mountain looming over Horseshoe Pond and beyond. To complete the hike, retrace your path to the trailhead.

3.0 Arrive back at the trailhead.

27 Rum Pond Loop

This hike starts at picturesque Rum Pond, with Big Moose Mountain visible across the pond. The trail crosses a ridge to reach Cranberry Pond; this remote pond is quite lovely. Access from the trail is on one of the many moose trails to the shoreline. This loop is little used; in fact, in most places the trail bed is solid wildflowers in season. This is a great hike for both wildlife and wildflowers.

Start: Rum Pond Trailhead, at west end of the parking area
Elevation gain: 583 feet
Distance: 3.4-mile loop
Hiking time: 2–3 hours
Difficulty: Easy
Season: May–Nov
Trail surface: Woodland path
Land status: Private forestland maintained by the State of Maine
Nearest town: Greenville
Other users: Hunters in season

Water availability: None
Canine compatibility: Dogs must be under control at all times.
Fees and permits: No fees or permits required
Maps: *DeLorme: Maine Atlas & Gazetteer:* Map 41; USGS Barren Mountain
Trail contact: None
Amenities available: None
Maximum grade: Average 10% grade for the 0.8-mile climb from Rum Pond to top of ridge
Cell service: None

Finding the trailhead: From the blinking light in downtown Greenville, drive north on Lily Bay Road. Less than 0.1 mile past the light, turn right onto Pleasant Street and drive 2.1 miles. The pavement ends as you drive around the airport. Continue another 1.6 miles, crossing Big Wilson Stream just below the dam. The road changes names to KI Road. Drive 2.5 miles, passing Morkill Road. Drive another 0.9 mile. Turn left onto Rum Pond Road at the sign for Rum Pond and drive 1 mile to the end of the road. Parking is on the left. The trailhead is at the back of the parking area. Trailhead GPS: N45° 27.859' / W69° 28.603'

The Hike

From the parking area, it's a short walk down to the shore of Rum Pond. The fishing here must be good, given the dozens of boats stashed in the woods along the shore. To the right of where the trail ends, a large boulder sits in the shallows. You can climb atop this rock and get a great view down the pond. Across the pond, you can see Big Moose Mountain.

From the pond, retrace your steps to the Blue Ridge Trail. This trail loops around the corner of the pond to the shore. Past this pond access, the trail climbs gently. You cross a hill between Blue Ridge and Rum Mountain. The trail then descends to the shore of Cranberry Pond.

There are several Cranberry Ponds in Maine. All are named for the wild fruit that grows on their marshy edges. There's no official access to this pond, but moose have

Cranberry Pond

created several trails; there's also a rough trail leading to a canoe on the shore. It's a pretty pond with irregular hills rising on the far side. The trail near the pond and the pond itself show evidence of regular moose activity. This is one of the most understated but scenic ponds in Maine.

Around the east end of the pond, you leave the Blue Ridge Trail (which continues to Notch Pond and is intended to continue over Blue Ridge to Hedgehog Gate on the KI Road). The Rum Brook Trail wanders through the woods, rising and falling with undulations of the land. In several places, no trail bed is visible because the forest floor is blanketed with wildflowers—mostly trout lilies in spring.

After passing a small brook, the trail climbs to a ridge. You pass the Headwaters Trail and partial views south. The Headwaters Trail wanders off the ridge and past a marshy brook, then loops around a clear-cut to end at a logging road within sight of KI Road just west of Vaughn Stream. For this hike, stay on the Rum Brook Trail.

The Rum Brook Trail descends gently off the ridge and ends at the Blue Ridge Trail almost within sight of the trailhead. The highlights of this hike are Cranberry Pond and all the wildflowers you wander through in season.

Along the shore of Rum Pond

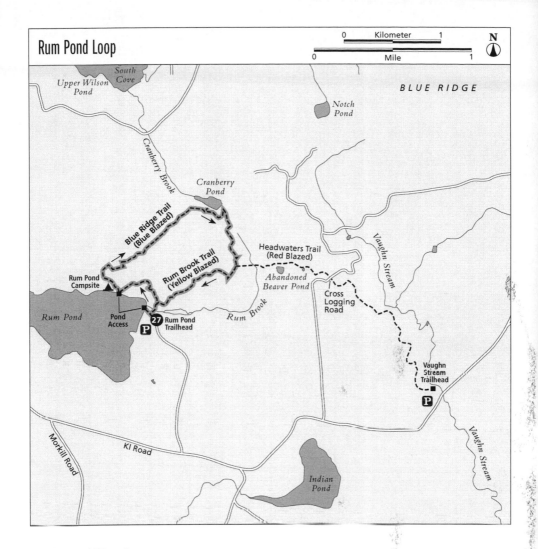

Miles and Directions

0.0 Start at the Rum Pond Trailhead.

0.1 Hike straight, passing a side trail to the shore of Rum Pond.

0.2 Retrace your steps to the junction and turn left onto the blue-blazed Blue Ridge Trail.

0.3 The trail jogs out onto a rough road to cross Rum Brook then reenters the woods. Pass the yellow-blazed Rum Brook Trail.

0.7 Pass a short side trail to Rum Pond.

1.0 Climb steadily away from Rum Pond onto a ridge.

1.9 Climb across the ridge, then descend to Cranberry Pond. Access to the pond is via one of several short side trails created by moose.

No trail bed, just a carpet of wildflowers

2.1   Hike around the east end of Cranberry Pond to a junction. Turn right onto the yellow-blazed Rum Brook Trail. (***Note:*** The Blue Ridge Trail continues another mile to Notch Pond. Plans are to extend the trail all the way to the AMC trails west of Lyford Ponds.)

2.6   Wander through wildflowers and climb gently. Pass the red-blazed Headwaters Trail. (***Note:*** The Headwaters Trail descends past a marshy stream then alongside a large clear-cut before ending in 2.1 miles at the KI Road near its crossing of Vaughn Stream.)

3.3   Descend off the ridge and wander through more wildflowers beneath hardwoods to a junction with the Blue Ridge Trail. Turn left.

3.4   Arrive back at the trailhead.

28 Hedgehog Mountain

This small mountain is in the middle of nowhere north of the White Cap Range near the West Branch Ponds. It's a nice hike through forest full of wildflowers and boulders. There are no views from the wooded summit, but the hike offers maximum solitude—a real tromp through Maine's wildness.

Start: Hedgehog Mountain Trailhead, on the north side of Frenchtown Road
Elevation gain: 829 feet
Distance: 3.2 miles out and back
Hiking time: About 2 hours
Difficulty: Easy
Season: June–Oct
Trail surface: Woodland path
Land status: AMC Maine Woods
Nearest town: Greenville
Other users: None
Water availability: None

Canine compatibility: Dogs must be under control at all times.
Fees and permits: No fees or permits required
Maps: *DeLorme: Maine Atlas & Gazetteer:* Map 42; USGS Hay Mountain
Trail contact: Appalachian Mountain Club; outdoors.org
Amenities available: None
Maximum grade: Average 16.6% grade on the 0.5 mile from the brook crossing to the summit, with two short steeper sections
Cell service: None

Finding the trailhead: From the blinking light in Greenville, drive north on Lily Bay Road for 17.7 miles. Just before reaching Kokadjo and Roach River, turn right onto Frenchtown Road and drive 9.9 miles. The signed trailhead is on the left. Park on the shoulder of the road. If you reach the turn for West Branch Pond Camps, you've gone 0.3 mile too far. Trailhead GPS: N45° 35.137' / W69° 17.797'

The Hike

Hedgehog Mountain sits north of the White Cap Range amid the ponds that are the origin of West Branch Pleasant River. It's an unassuming little mountain of just over 2,000 feet. The trail climbs gently away from Frenchtown Road. You pass through forest with boulders here and there. In season, wildflowers add color to the woods.

After crossing a small brook, the trail climbs more steadily. The ground is ledgy. The pathway teases you with partial views west and south. The topography makes it seem like there's going to be a better view just ahead—several times—but no open views materialize. You climb through big trees towering over a hanging meadow.

The trail levels out and ends at the rock pile on the summit. As with the climb, it appears that a short bushwhack in any direction will lead to a view. This is just an illusion created by the slopes populated with hardwoods. Even though there's no view, the process of climbing this small mountain offers its own rewards. The babbling brook, the profusion of wildflowers, the big trees, and the boulders in the woods all make for a pleasant walk.

A bit of climbing

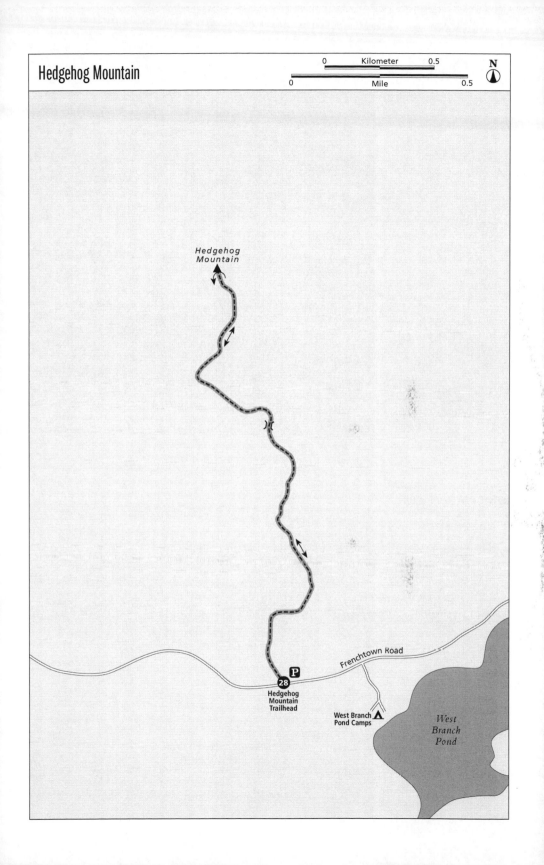

Hedgehog Mountain

0   Kilometer   0.5

0   Mile   0.5

N

Hedgehog
Mountain

Frenchtown Road

P

28

Hedgehog
Mountain
Trailhead

West Branch
Pond Camps

West
Branch
Pond

The wooded summit

Miles and Directions

0.0 Start at the Hedgehog Mountain Trailhead.

0.9 Climb gently through woods to a small brook.

1.6 Climb more steadily, with some partial views to the wooded summit. To complete the hike, retrace your steps to the trailhead.

3.2 Arrive back at the trailhead.

29 Shaw Mountain

Shaw Mountain sits by itself between First and Second Roach Ponds. Its north peak is wooded but still a nice hike. The middle peak is also wooded, but the trail to it passes two overlooks with spectacular views. The rocky woods of the summit ridge make a good place to see spring wildflowers such as trilliums and lady's slippers.

Start: Shaw Mountain Trailhead, on north side of Lower Crossover Road
Elevation gain: 1,281 feet
Distance: 3.6 miles out and back
Hiking time: 3–4 hours
Difficulty: Moderate
Season: June–Oct
Trail surface: Woodland path
Land status: AMC North Woods
Nearest town: Greenville
Other users: None
Water availability: Shaw Brook

Canine compatibility: Dogs must be under control at all times.
Fees and permits: No fees or permits required
Maps: *DeLorme: Maine Atlas & Gazetteer:* Map 42; USGS Farrar Mountain
Trail contact: Appalachian Mountain Club; outdoors.org
Amenities available: None
Maximum grade: Average 15% grade on the climb from the trailhead to the summit ridge, with steeper sections on the mountain bike trail and after leaving that trail
Cell service: None

Finding the trailhead: From the blinking light in Greenville, drive north on Lily Bay Road. The pavement ends at Kokadjo after 18.5 miles; continue driving for 0.4 mile. Bear left at the fork onto Sias Hill Road and drive 0.9 mile. Pass an intersection and continue 0.4 mile. Turn right onto Smithtown Road and drive 4.8 miles, passing Nahmakanta Road. Continue 2.8 miles, passing the entrance to AMC's Medawisla Lodge. Turn right onto Lower Crossover Road (sometimes called Shaw Mountain Road) and drive 0.4 mile. Bear right at the intersection and continue 0.5 mile. Park on the right just across the bridge over Shaw Brook. The trailhead is across the road from the parking area. Trailhead GPS: N45° 39.273' / W69° 18.683'

The Hike

The AMC has developed ski, biking, and hiking trails centered on its Medawisla Lodge on Second Roach Pond. The remote trail up Shaw Mountain is one of them. The trail begins by climbing gently beside Shaw Brook through mixed forest. In less than 0.5 mile the trail climbs a hillock beside the brook and leaves it. You climb steadily to a mountain biking trail. Turn left onto that trail—really a wide gravel logging road. Climb steadily to where the trail bears right off the road.

From here you climb more steeply through rock forest to another crossing of the mountain bike trail. If you look to your left, you can see where the bike trail loops through a small cirque. It would add a little bit your hike, but on your descent, you may want to take the mountain bike trail down to walk across the floor of the cirque.

Katahdin from the first overlook

Past the mountain bike trail, it's a short, steady climb to the shoulder between the north and middle peaks of Shaw Mountain. Turn right at the junction and climb gently to the wooded north peak. Return to the junction and hike southeast toward the middle peak. You pass an overlook with a great view of Katahdin and the line of mountains in Baxter State Park. This is a great spot to find a boulder where you can perch and eat lunch.

The trail then wanders across the summit ridge through spruces, with lots of greenery beneath them, especially bluebead lilies. Just before the middle peak, there's another overlook. From here you can see Katahdin, with Second Roach Pond beneath you. The summit is just behind you: a bare ledge in the woods surrounded by spruce.

The trail continues past the summit for about 0.5 mile. The AMC intends to continue this trail off Shaw Mountain and across the valley to Hedgehog Mountain. There are no views along the trail so far, but the last time I visited, I did encounter a spruce grouse, watching me curiously from a tree beside the trail.

Middle peak of Shaw Mountain

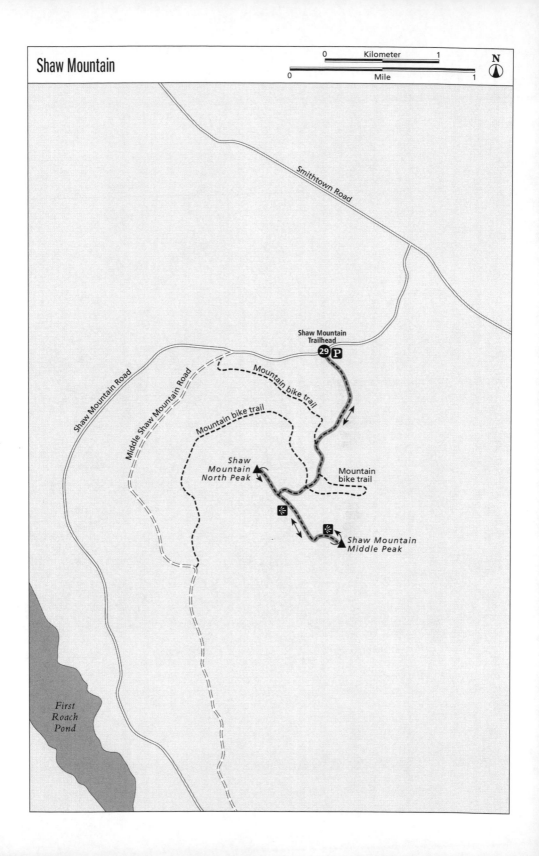

Shaw Mountain

Smithtown Road

Shaw Mountain Road

Middle Shaw Mountain Road

Mountain bike trail

Mountain bike trail

Mountain bike trail

Shaw Mountain Trailhead

29 P

Shaw Mountain North Peak

Shaw Mountain Middle Peak

First Roach Pond

N

0   Kilometer   1

0   Mile   1

Miles and Directions

0.0 Start at the Shaw Mountain Trailhead.

0.3 Climb gently beside Shaw Brook. Leave the brook and begin to climb more steadily.

0.6 Climb steadily to a wide gravel mountain bike trail. Turn left onto the gravel trail.

0.7 Climb steadily on the gravel trail then bear right onto the hiking trail.

0.9 Cross the mountain bike trail.

1.1 Climb steadily to the saddle between Shaw Mountain's summits. Turn right at the junction.

1.3 Climb gently to the wooded north summit. Retrace your steps to the junction in the saddle.

1.5 Bear right at the junction.

1.6 Climb steadily to an overlook.

1.9 Climb gently to another overlook. The trail turns right.

2.0 Reach the middle summit. (*Note:* The summit is unsigned, and the trail continues beyond the summit for 0.5 mile. Eventually the trail will go all the way to Hedgehog Mountain.) To complete the hike, retrace your steps to the junction in the saddle.

2.4 Arrive back at the junction. Turn right and retrace your steps to the trailhead.

3.6 Arrive back at the trailhead.

30 Indian Falls

Indian Falls is only a few miles from Little Wilson Falls as the crow flies. Both waterfalls are significant drops where small streams enter Big Wilson Stream's steep-sided slate valley. Indian Falls is reached by following an abandoned roadbed to a short trail that leads to the falls. The falls drop over black slate, surrounded by towering evergreens—one of the most scenic waterfalls in Maine.

Start: Where Indian Falls Road becomes too overgrown to drive
Distance: 2.2 miles out and back
Elevation gain: 320 feet
Hiking time: About 2 hours
Difficulty: Easy
Season: Best May–Oct
Trail surface: Woodland path and abandoned road
Land status: Commercial timberland
Nearest town: Greenville
Other users: Hunters in season

Water availability: Indian Stream
Canine compatibility: Dogs must be under control at all times.
Fees and permits: No fees or permits required
Maps: *DeLorme: Maine Atlas & Gazetteer:* Map 41; USGS Barren Mountain West
Trail contact: None
Amenities available: None
Maximum grade: The last 0.2 mile to the base of the waterfall descends at a 10% grade.
Cell service: None

Finding the trailhead: From the blinking light in Greenville, drive north on Lily Bay Road less than 0.1 mile. Turn right onto Pleasant Street and drive 2.1 miles to where the pavement ends as you drive around the airport. Continue another 1.6 miles. The road crosses Big Wilson Stream and becomes the KI Road. Drive another 2.5 miles. Turn right onto Morkill Road at the sign and continue 1.6 miles. Bear left at the fork, staying on Morkill Road, and drive 1.1 miles, passing a recent cut and beginning to go down a hill with a view of Barren Mountain in the distance. Turn right onto Indian Falls Road, a small narrow road. You can park at the top and walk down to the trailhead or drive 0.1 mile to a wide grassy area to park. Do not drive all the way to the end of the road. The road ends at the railroad tracks but is no longer passable by car. The hike follows the road to and across the railroad tracks. Trailhead GPS: N45° 25.346' / W69° 28.496'

The Hike

Full disclosure: My family and I spent the better part of a morning driving around on logging roads looking for the Indian Falls Trailhead. You can avoid an adventure like ours by carefully following the driving directions above. Because of the number of logging roads and dearth of road signs, this hike more than any of the others in this guide requires that you keep track of the mileage between turns on your way from Greenville to the trailhead.

As we were driving around, my wife suggested that Indian Falls shouldn't be in this guide—it was too hard to find. When we walked past the trail to the falls

Indian Falls

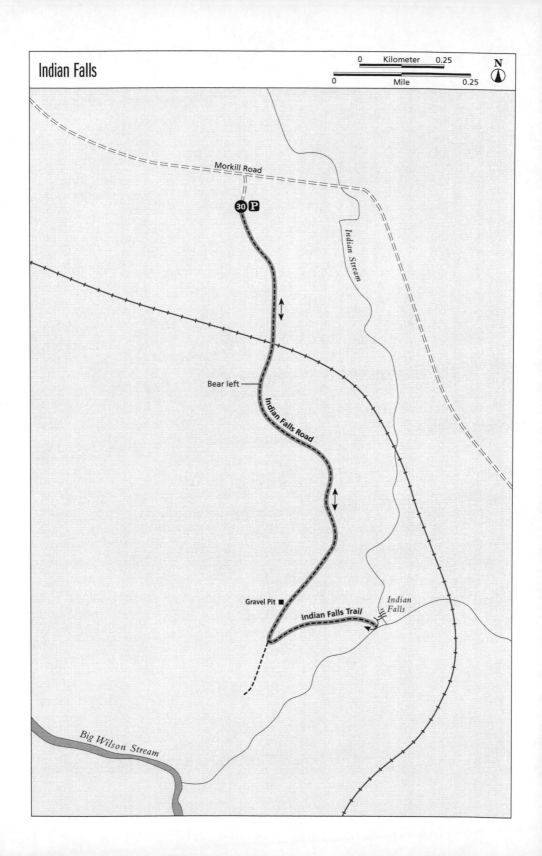

Indian Falls

0   Kilometer   0.25

0   Mile   0.25

N

Morkill Road

30 P

Indian Stream

Bear left

Indian Falls Road

Gravel Pit ■

Indian Falls Trail

Indian Falls

Big Wilson Stream

Indian Falls

and followed the roadbed too far down toward Big Wilson Stream, she adamantly repeated her opinion.

But when we made it to the base of the falls, she changed her mind, asserting that it absolutely needed to be in the guide. Indian Falls drops 60 feet down a black slate face, following seams in the bedrock in several horsetails. The water crashes off joints in the rock, creating a chaotic pattern of dancing mist that dampens both the surrounding forest and hikers gaping at the falls.

Find a flat rock to bask on like a lizard, soaking up the warm summer sun and the white noise of water beating on slate. Or explore the rock face around the falls, viewing it from different angles. The stream above the falls is worth a look. It pools among jumbled boulders, slides down water-smoothed bedrock, and jumps into the air, sparkling with kinetic energy.

Miles and Directions

0.0 Start 0.1 mile from Morkill Road. Follow the road downhill to the railroad tracks.

0.2 Cross the railroad tracks and following a narrow trail through an alder thicket.

0.3 Bear left in an open area that used to be an intersection; climb a gentle rise.

0.7 Descend off the rise and pass a gravel pit. The trail to this point is very overgrown. The trail is easy to follow, but alders and birches have overgrown the old roadbed.

0.8 Turn left at a cairn onto the Indian Falls Trail, following the red flagging. (The roadbed continues downhill all the way to Big Wilson Stream.)

1.1 Arrive at Indian Falls. You can easily reach both the top and base of the falls. To complete the hike, return the way you came.

2.2 Arrive back at the trailhead.

31 Little Lyford Ponds

This hike follows the Laurie's Ledge Trail down from the trailhead to the Nation's Nature Trail. The nature trail is an easy loop that visits many of the area's highlights. On this hike you visit First Little Lyford Pond, the AMC lodge, the historic trail to the camps, The Pinnacle, and Marian Rock.

Start: Indian Mountain
Distance: 1.9-mile lollipop
Elevation gain: 357 feet
Hiking time: About 2 hours
Difficulty: Easy
Season: Best May–Oct
Trail surface: Woodland path
Land status: AMC Recreation and Conservation Area
Nearest town: Greenville
Other users: None
Water availability: First Little Lyford Pond and Pleasant River

Canine compatibility: Dogs must be on a leash at all times.
Fees and permits: Access fee paid at the Hedgehog gate on the KI Road
Maps: *DeLorme: Maine Atlas & Gazetteer:* Map 41; USGS Hay Mountain
Trail contact: Appalachian Mountain Club, Greenville Office; (207) 695-3085; outdoors.org
Amenities available: Water and information at the lodge
Maximum grade: 6.6% grade for the short, 0.3-mile climb to The Pinnacle
Cell service: None

Finding the trailhead: From the blinking light in Greenville, drive north on Lily Bay Road. Almost immediately turn right onto Pleasant Street. As you leave Greenville, the road becomes East Road. The pavement ends at the airport. At Lower Wilson Pond, the road becomes the KI Road. There are numerous side roads, which change from year to year depending on the needs of the logging companies. The AMC has put up signs directing you to their lodges at most side roads. Follow the signs, staying on the KI Road. At 12.1 miles from the blinking light in Greenville, you reach the Hedgehog gate, where you need to pay the fee. Past the gate, drive 2.9 miles then turn left onto Upper Valley Road. Continue 2.3 miles to the trailhead parking, on the left. Cross the road from the parking area to the Laurie's Ledge Trailhead. Trailhead GPS: N45° 31.034' / W69° 21.922'

The Hike

Little Lyford Camps were famous for their remote location and the fishing. Since the Appalachian Mountain Club purchased the camps and 60,000 acres surrounding them, the area has become known for its cross-country skiing and hiking.

The Nation's Nature Trail is an easy loop that visits many of the area's most historic and scenic features. After descending from the trailhead on the Laurie's Ledge Trail, you arrive at the nature trail, where several large, angular boulders lie in the forest like a large organic sculpture. The boulders probably fell all the way from the cliffs high on Indian Mountain, which the trail to Laurie's Ledge passes.

First Little Lyford Pond

The nature trail heads north through the woods toward First Little Lyford Pond. The trail passes within sight of the pond. Don't bushwhack to it; you'll shortly reach the shore on the Prior's Path.

The Prior's Path crosses a marshy meadow where First Little Lyford Pond's outlet stream winds, unhurried, to the Pleasant River. The trail ends at a dock on the pond. The sign at the trailhead gives distance to both First and Second Little Lyford Ponds. But except when the ponds are frozen, this is the end of the trail. Across the pond, Indian and Elephant Mountains jut from the deep green forest.

Past the Prior's Path, the nature trail passes through the camps. You can take a short side trip to the main lodge and check out their maps and exhibits. The staff is always happy to answer your questions.

The hike reenters the woods on the historic trail—the route that generations of visitors followed to the camps. This wide, low trail follows the Pleasant River and can be used to connect to the Gulf Hagas trails. The nature trail turns away from the river and the historic trail and climbs gently to The Pinnacle. This rocky outcropping offers very limited views across the Pleasant River valley.

Before crossing the camp road and arriving back at the Laurie's Ledge Trail, the nature trail passes a large erratic boulder called Marian Rock.

Little Lyford Ponds

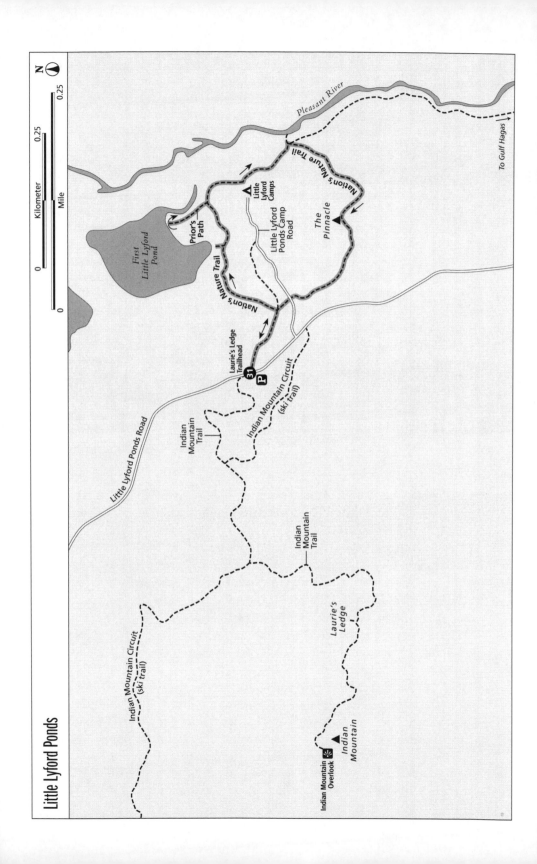

N

Kilometer
0   0.25

Mile
0   0.25

First Little Lyford Pond

Prior's Path

Pleasant River

Little Lyford Camps

Little Lyford Ponds Camp Road

Nation's Nature Trail

The Pinnacle

To Gulf Hagas

Nation's Nature Trail

Laurie's Ledge Trailhead

31

P

Little Lyford Ponds Road

Indian Mountain Trail

Indian Mountain Circuit (ski trail)

Indian Mountain Trail

Laurie's Ledge

Indian Mountain Circuit (ski trail)

Indian Mountain Overlook

Indian Mountain

Little Lyford Ponds Outlet

Miles and Directions

0.0 Start at the Laurie's Ledge Trailhead. Cross Little Lyford Ponds Road and follow the Laurie's Ledge Trail toward Little Lyford Ponds Camps.

0.2 At a large broken erratic boulder, turn left onto the Nation's Nature Trail.

0.4 Pass First Little Lyford Pond.

0.5 Pass an unmarked trail on the right that leads to the lodge.

0.6 Turn left onto the Prior's Path.

0.7 The Prior's Path ends at First Little Lyford Pond. To continue the hike, return to the nature trail.

0.8 Turn left onto the nature trail.

0.9 The nature trail emerges from the woods and crosses through the lodge and cabin area. Reenter the woods of the historic trail toward Gulf Hagas.

1.0 A side trail leads left 200 feet to the Pleasant River. Turn right onto the nature trail.

1.3 Turn right and begin to climb. Do not follow the yellow blazes straight.

1.4 On the right is The Pinnacle, a small open area with limited views.

1.6 Pass a very large erratic boulder known as Marian Rock.

1.7 Cross the camp road. In another 200 feet, arrive back at the Laurie's Ledge Trail. Turn left to return to the trailhead.

1.9 Arrive back at the trailhead.

32 Gulf Hagas from the West

Gulf Hagas is one of Maine's deepest canyons. The hike follows the West Branch Pleasant River as it drops 400 feet in 4 miles through the gulf. There are numerous waterfalls and rapids. The walls of the gulf rise vertically, at times as much as 140 feet high. Below Gulf Hagas, the hike follows Gulf Hagas Stream up past several waterfalls, including Screw Auger Falls—the highest on the whole hike.

Start: Head of the Gulf Trailhead, next to the large information sign across the road from the parking area

Distance: 10.2-mile lollipop

Elevation gain: 1,696 feet

Hiking time: 5–8 hours

Difficulty: Strenuous because of the distance

Season: Best mid-May–Oct, especially after heavy rains, when river levels are highest

Trail surface: Woodland path

Land status: Appalachian Mountain Club North Woods Recreation and Conservation Area and Appalachian Trail corridor

Nearest town: Greenville

Other users: None

Water availability: West Branch Pleasant River at 0.5 and 2.0 miles; Gulf Hagas Stream at 5.8 and 6.1 miles

Canine compatibility: Dogs must be under control at all times.

Fees and permits: Access fee paid at the Hedgehog gate on the KI Road

Maps: *DeLorme: Maine Atlas & Gazetteer:* Maps 41 and 42; USGS Barren Mountain East

Trail contact: Appalachian Mountain Club, Greenville Office; (207) 695-3085; outdoors.org
    Maine Appalachian Trail Club; matc.org
    KI Jo-Mary Forest; (207) 435-6213; northmainewoods.org

Amenities available: Outhouse at the trailhead

Maximum grade: For a flat hike, there's a remarkable amount of elevation change. There are no sustained climbs but lots of short ups and downs; some are as steep as 40% grade but most are less than 15%.

Cell service: None

Finding the trailhead: From the blinking light in Greenville, drive north on Lily Bay Road. Almost immediately turn right onto Pleasant Street. As you leave Greenville, the road becomes East Road. The pavement ends at the airport. At Lower Wilson Pond, the road becomes the KI Road. There are numerous side roads, which change from year to year depending on the needs of the logging companies. The AMC has put up signs directing you to their lodges at most side roads. Follow the signs, staying on the KI Road. At 12.1 miles from the blinking light in Greenville, you reach the Hedgehog gate, where you need to pay the fee. Past the gate, drive 2.9 miles. Turn left onto Little Lyford Ponds Road and drive 0.9 mile to the Head of the Gulf parking area, on the left just past the trailhead. Trailhead GPS: N45° 29.908' / W69° 21.418'

The Hike

No one is sure of the origin of the name Gulf Hagas. It has been suggested that it is a corruption of an Abenaki word or phrase, but the Penobscot name for Gulf Hagas is *Mahkonlahgok*, which doesn't seem to lend itself to being corrupted to "Gulf Hagas" by the nineteenth-century loggers who named it. In the White Mountains there

Stair Falls in low water

are several "gulfs"—a word usually associated with oceans but used in the names of cirques to describe the large empty space created by glaciers. Gulf Hagas is Maine's best known and deepest canyon, so calling it a gulf makes a certain amount of sense. But "hagas," because it is a homophone of "haggis," sounds Gaelic. "Haggis" does mean "chopped," so maybe there is a connection. It seems as reasonable an explanation as the corruption of an Abenaki term. Whatever the origin of its name, Gulf Hagas is one of Maine's natural wonders.

The West Branch Pleasant River flows through the 4-mile-long canyon, dropping almost 400 feet. The walls of the gulf are slate and at times rise vertically from the river for more than 100 feet. In places the canyon is less than 20 feet across. It was less than 8 feet wide at The Jaws until loggers blasted away rock, making it more than 20 feet wide. They widened the spot so that logs floated down the river in the spring freshet to Katahdin Iron Works wouldn't get jammed up at The Jaws. This was a dangerous stretch of river for the loggers; at least one river driver is known to have been killed in Gulf Hagas.

The hike begins at the west of the gulf along the river, which runs deep and silent above the Head of the Gulf. In addition to the west end of the gulf being generally less crowded, the advantage of beginning the hike here rather than at the Gulf Hagas Trailhead you passed on your drive in is that you avoid both of the river fords. Coming in from the east requires fording the West Branch Pleasant River below the gulf.

Buttermilk Falls

The crossing is more than 100 feet across, and the river bottom is slippery, round rocks. The water is usually cold enough to numb your calves and feet. Only in the driest times can the ford be done by hopping from rock to rock. When the river is that low, the falls in the gulf are much less dramatic. You also have to ford Gulf Hagas Brook above Screw Auger Falls. This crossing is only 30 feet wide, but it's deeper. Many folks that hike in from the east don't make it much past Screw Auger Falls.

At the Head of the Gulf, the West Branch Pleasant River and Bear Brook come together and separately drop into a large pool. The river then drops twice in quick succession as it makes a sharp bend to the east; this is Stair Falls. Several side trails off the Rim Trail allow you to climb around on the rock along the river. Below Stair Falls the gulf gets deeper and deeper. The steep, at times sheer, sides of the canyon are overhung with spruce and cedar trees. The river churns over rocks on its way to Billings Falls.

There is a short side trail out to the top of Billings Falls. You can stand on the uneven rock and look straight down on the river as it plunges into a large pool. Farther along the Rim Trail is an overlook from across that pool looking toward Billings Falls. After following along the gulf for another mile, the canyon varying from 50 to

The Jaws

140 feet deep with rapid after rapid, you come to Buttermilk Falls. As at Billings Falls, there is an overlook above the falls and another looking back at it.

At Buttermilk Falls, a cutoff trail leads to the Pleasant River Road Trail. This way, you can make a shorter hike of the west end of Gulf Hagas. Then, on another day, you can hike the east end from the other trailhead.

Below Buttermilk Falls, the walls of the gulf narrow and are more vertical. Along this section are the two narrow pinches known as The Jaws. A side trail leads down to an overlook above the river a short distance from The Jaws. Past The Jaws, a side trail leads down to the river at Cole's Corner, where you can look back upstream through the narrowest part of the canyon. An area of quiet water here is often used as a swimming hole in summer. During the spring, the water is too high and moves too fast.

After Cole's Corner, the Rim Trail climbs up and away from the gulf. The forest changes from evergreens to hardwoods. The canyon is at its deepest here, but the sides are somewhat less vertical. A side trail leads to an overlook above Hammond Street Pitch, named for the street in Bangor. Most of the loggers spent the winter in the woods, cutting and hauling wood. After the logs were floated down the river, the loggers made their way to Bangor to spend their wages. At that time, Bangor was a wild frontier town of great wealth. With all the taverns and entertainments for the loggers, it was considered unsafe for women. A logger who remembered stumbling down Hammond Street as it dropped toward downtown must have been inspired to name Hammond Street Pitch.

The Rim Trail leaves the Pleasant River and follows Gulf Hagas Stream up past several waterfalls. There are side trails to the lower falls and to Screw Auger Falls. In the 0.3 mile the trail follows Gulf Hagas Stream, the stream drops 150 feet. Above Screw Auger Falls, the Rim Trail ends. To the right, across the stream, is the Appalachian Trail, leading to the Gulf Hagas Trailhead. To the left, 4 miles west on the Pleasant River Road Trail, is the Head of Gulf Trailhead, where you started.

Miles and Directions

0.0   Start at the Head of the Gulf Trailhead, across the road from the parking area.

0.5   Follow the Head of the Gulf Trail to a gravel road. Turn right and cross the West Branch Pleasant River.

0.6   At a cairn and a sign, the trail turns right and leaves the road.

1.0   The trail skirts around the west and south shores of Lloyd Pond; there is a 100-foot-long side trail to the pond.

1.9   The Head of the Gulf Trail ends at the junction with the Pleasant River Road and Gulf Hagas Rim Trails. Turn right onto the Gulf Hagas Rim Trail.

2.0   Reach Head of the Gulf. There is a short side trail out onto the rocks at the top of Stair Falls. (**Note:** All signs for side trails on Gulf Hagas Rim Trail face away from you as you hike.) Most side trails have an upstream and downstream connection to the Rim Trail, with the sign near the downstream side trail. On this hike, you will mostly use the upstream, up-marked side trails.

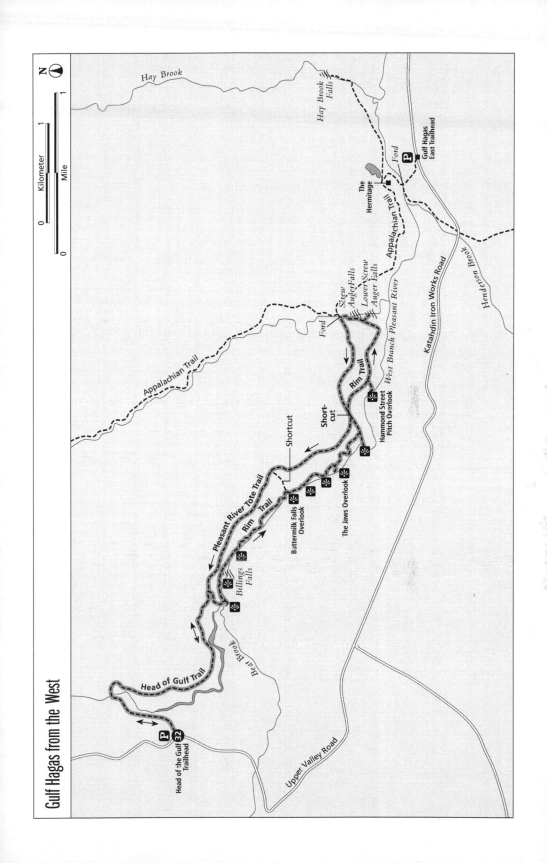

Gulf Hagas from the West

2.1 A side trail leads out onto the rocks below Stair Falls.

2.2 A short side trail leads to a cliff top directly above Billings Falls.

2.3 A side trail leads 150 feet to an overlook with a view upstream to Billings Falls.

3.3 After Billings Falls, numerous unmarked side trails lead to overlooks and cliff tops, all worth exploring. Arrive at a cliff-top overlook of Buttermilk Falls.

3.4 Reach a junction with a cutoff trail that leads in 0.6 mile to the Pleasant River Road Trail. To continue the hike, go straight on the Rim Trail. (**Option:** You can shorten the hike to 6.7 miles by taking this cutoff and then turning left onto the Pleasant River Road Trail.)

3.7 After the cutoff trail, the Rim Trail passes several short side trails to overlooks. This section of the gulf is particularly deep and narrow. The last of these side trails is just upstream of The Jaws.

4.0 A side trail leads 0.1 mile down to the river, where there is a view upstream of The Jaws. At The Jaws, the walls of the canyon are only 18 feet apart.

4.8 Reach a junction with a second cutoff trail to the Pleasant River Road Trail. (**Option:** Take the cutoff and return to the trailhead for an 8.4-mile hike.) To continue, stay on the Rim Trail.

5.0 A 0.1-mile side trail leads to an overlook of Hammond Street Pitch, the deepest section of the gulf. The trail appears to continue up and away from the cliff, but it peters out above a rocky area.

5.7 Past Hammond Street Pitch, the Rim Trail turns away from the rim of the gulf and passes through a hardwood forest to a side trail that leads 0.1 mile to the lower falls on Gulf Hagas Brook.

5.9 A short side trail leads to an overlook of Screw Auger Falls. You can climb down from the overlook to the pool between the two falls.

6.0 The trail passes along the rocks at the top of Screw Auger Falls.

6.1 The Gulf Hagas Rim Trail ends at the junction of the Pleasant River Road Trail and the trail across Gulf Hagas Stream that leads to the Appalachian Trail and the main Gulf Hagas trailhead. Turn left onto the Pleasant River Road Trail.

6.7 Pass the second cutoff trail.

7.5 Cross the first cutoff trail.

8.3 Arrive back at the Head of the Gulf Trail. Go straight and retrace your steps to the trailhead.

10.2 Arrive back at the trailhead.

33 Gulf Hagas from the East

This hike follows the most popular route into Gulf Hagas. You ford Pleasant River, hike around The Hermitage—a stand of old-growth white pines, then hike the Appalachian Trail to Gulf Hagas. You begin the loop by passing Screw Auger Falls. The Rim Trail then follows upstream along the river through the gorge, passing many side trails to waterfalls, overlooks, and other features. Gulf Hagas is Maine's most famous canyon, a deep slate gorge 4 miles long.

Start: Gulf Hagas east trailhead
Elevation gain: 1,850 feet
Distance: 9.3-mile lollipop
Hiking time: About 8 hours
Difficulty: Strenuous
Season: Late May–Oct
Trail surface: Woodland path with two stream fords
Land Status: Appalachian Trail corridor
Nearest town: Brownville
Other users: None
Water availability: Gulf Hagas Brook at 1.6 miles
Canine compatibility: Dogs must be under control at all times.

Fees and permits: Access fee paid at the Katahdin Iron Works gate
Maps: *DeLorme: Maine Atlas & Gazetteer:* Maps 41 and 42; USGS Barren Mountain East
Trail contact: North Maine Woods, Inc.; (207) 435-6213
Amenities available: Outhouse at trailhead
Maximum grade: For a flat hike, there's a remarkable amount of elevation change. There are no sustained climbs but lots of short ups and downs; some are as steep as 40% grade but most are less than 15%.
Cell service: None

Finding the trailhead: From the bridge over the Pleasant River in Brownville, follow ME 11 north for 4.8 miles. Turn left onto the KI Road at the sign for Katahdin Iron Works and Gulf Hagas. Drive 6.5 miles to the gate, where you pay your fee. Cross the Pleasant River and turn right. Drive 3.5 miles to a fork in the road; take the left fork, following the signs to Gulf Hagas. Drive 2.9 miles; the parking area is on the right at the sign for Gulf Hagas. Trailhead GPS: N45° 28.667' / W69° 17.122'

The Hike

The hike begins with a ford of Pleasant River. I once made it all the way across on rocks until the last 10 feet. I had to balance on a rock in the river and take off one of my shoes. Usually, that doesn't work. Most of the year, you'll have to wade across the shin- to knee-deep river. The riverbed is slippery, rounded rocks, so it's best to bring water shoes for the crossing.

Across the river, the trail winds around then passes through The Hermitage, a stand of old-growth white pines. After that, you wander through the rocky woods, hearing the river on your left. Where the Appalachian Trail turns right to climb the White Cap Range, you go straight and ford Gulf Hagas Brook. This ford is only 20 feet across, but it's usually deeper than the earlier river crossing.

Emma skipping through The Hermitage

Screw Auger Falls

From there you can see the top of Screw Auger Falls—actually two falls with a pool between them tucked into a narrow slate gorge. Side trails lead to overlooks of each fall and to the base of the lower one. Getting to the base requires a bit of rock scrambling, but the view is worth it. There's also a nice swimming hole there.

A little farther downstream, a marked side trail leads to Lower Screw Auger Falls. This waterfall is a long, picturesque slide. Below this waterfall, Gulf Hagas Brook flows into the Pleasant River as it emerges from Gulf Hagas. The trail climbs to the rim of the canyon and follows it upstream.

The first side trail you'll come to leads to a ledgy cliff top with a view of the deepest part of the canyon and Hammond Street Pitch. The next side trail leads to a cliff-top overlook of Cole's Corner. Here the canyon is narrower and steeper. After that, you'll come to a side trail that leads down into the canyon just downstream from The Jaws. As you descend this trail, you'll come to an unmarked fork. Going straight leads down to the boulders along the river (a good swimming hole when the water is low). To the right, the blazed trail leads to the top of a boulder overlooking the river. You can clearly see The Jaws upstream. It's the narrowest point in the canyon. It was originally a mere 12 feet across, but loggers blasted it to 20 feet to facilitate their log runs.

Upstream from The Jaws, the Rim Trail crosses more open ledges with views of the canyon. You have wonderful views of the river and the vertical slate bedding on the far side. This section feels a lot more like being in a canyon than earlier in the hike. You reach a high cliff-top overlook of Buttermilk Falls. Just past that overlook, you pass the cutoff trail. You can use this to shorten the hike. Since the complete hike is more than 9 miles from either end, it makes a certain amount of sense to hike each end separately, using the cutoff each time.

Past the cutoff, you'll pass an overlook at the top of Buttermilk Falls. The Rim Trail remains ledgy, with lots of overlooks. Come to Billings Falls. As with Buttermilk Falls, there's an overlook below and above the falls. A short distance farther, you'll reach Stair Falls. Here the river makes a wide bend. There's good access here to the wide ledges with views of the several falls that make up Stairs Falls. The top of Stair Falls, where Bear Brook drops into the river, is Head of the Gulf. Turn right onto the Pleasant River Road Trail and follow it back to the ford over Gulf Hagas Brook. This is an easy walk along an old roadbed through hardwoods—a good place to find lots of wildflowers and, on quiet days, even a moose.

Miles and Directions

0.0 Start at the Gulf Hagas east trailhead.

0.2 Pass the southbound AT and ford Pleasant River.

0.4 Loop around The Hermitage. Turn left at a junction, staying on the northbound AT.

1.6 Go straight when the AT turns left. Ford Gulf Hagas Brook.

1.7 Across the brook, turn left onto the Rim Trail and reach the top of Screw Auger Falls.

1.9 A side trail leads to view of Screw Auger Falls. Turn right onto the side trail.

2.0 The trail seems to end at a precarious overlook, but it continues down the rock face to the base of Screw Auger Falls. To continue the hike, retrace your steps to the Rim Trail. Turn left, back onto the Rim Trail.

2.1 Turn left onto a side trail to Lower Screw Auger Falls.

2.2 Reach Lower Screw Auger Falls. To continue the hike, retrace your steps to the Rim Trail.

2.3 Turn left, back on the Rim Trail.

2.7 Turn left on a side trail to the Hammond Street Pitch overlook.

2.8 Reach the overlook. To continue the hike, retrace your steps to the Rim Trail.

2.9 Turn left, back onto the Rim Trail.

3.3 Turn left onto a side trail to Cole's Corner.

3.4 Reach an overlook. To continue the hike, retrace your steps to the Rim Trail.

3.5 Turn left, back onto the Rim Trail.

3.8 Turn left onto a side trail to The Jaws.

3.9 The side trail forks. The straight-ahead fork descends to the river below The Jaws. The right forks ends at an overlook of The Jaws. To continue the hike, retrace your steps to the Rim Trail.

4.0 Turn left, back onto the Rim Trail.

4.2 Cross ledges with a fine view.

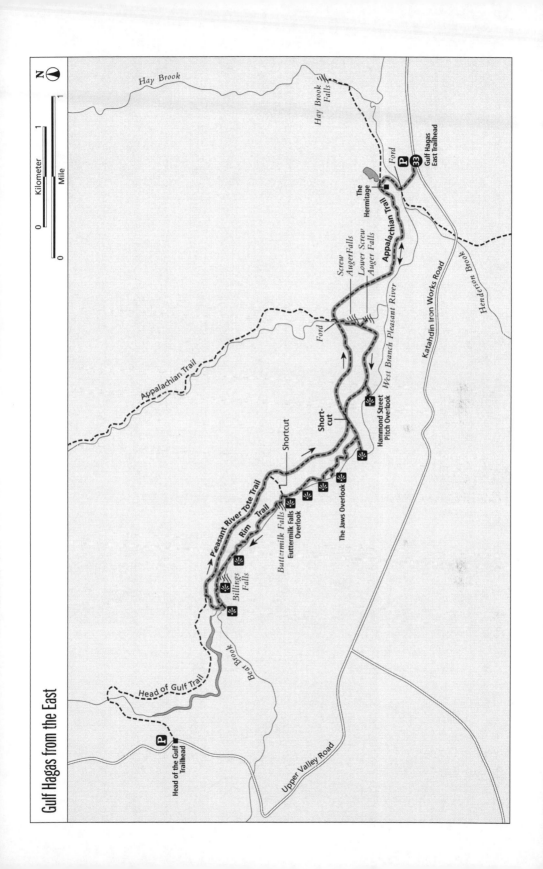

Gulf Hagas from the East

N

1 Kilometer

1 Mile

Hay Brook

Hay Brook Falls

Ford

P

33

Gulf Hagas East Trailhead

The Hermitage

Appalachian Trail

Screw Auger Falls

Lower Screw Auger Falls

Ford

West Branch Pleasant River

Katahdin Iron Works Road

Henderson Brook

Appalachian Trail

Shortcut

Shortcut

Hammond Street Pitch Overlook

Pleasant River Tote Trail

Rim Trail

Buttermilk Falls

Buttermilk Falls Overlook

The Jaws Overlook

Billings Falls

Head of Gulf Trail

Gulf Brook

P

Head of the Gulf Trailhead

Upper Valley Road

Lower Screw Auger Falls

4.4 Cross ledges with a view of Buttermilk Falls. Pass a cutoff trail. (**Option:** Turn right onto the cutoff and take it to the Pleasant River Road Trail. Turn right on that trail and take it back to the Gulf Hagas Brook ford for a loop of 7.7 miles.)

4.5 Pass the top of Buttermilk Falls.

5.5 The trail passes several overlooks and reaches a side trail that leads 150 feet to an overlook of Billings Falls.

5.6 Pass the top of Billings Falls.

5.7 Pass a side trail to the base of Stair Falls.

5.8 Pass several access points to rocks along Stair Falls, then reach Head of the Gulf. Turn right onto the Pleasant River Road Trail.

6.4 Cross the cutoff trail.

7.7 Arrive back at the Gulf Hagas Brook ford. Cross the brook and retrace your steps to the trailhead.

9.3 Arrive back at the trailhead.

34 Henderson Brook

This easy hike follows Henderson Brook from where it drops out of a boggy valley and races through a narrow canyon. The trail crisscrosses the stream as it flows against one then the other side of the canyon. You can follow the trail all the way out to the KI Road or hike as far as the last stream crossing and return the way you came.

Start: Henderson Brook Trailhead, between the parking area and the bridge over Henderson Brook

Distance: 1.8 miles out and back or 1.1-mile shuttle

Elevation gain: 501 feet

Hiking time: 1-2 hours

Difficulty: Easy

Season: Best May–Oct

Trail surface: Woodland path

Land status: AMC Recreation and Conservation Area and Appalachian Trail

Nearest town: Greenville

Other users: Hunters in season

Water availability: Henderson Brook

Canine compatibility: Dogs must be under control at all times.

Fees and permits: Access fee paid at the Hedgehog gate on the KI Road

Maps: *DeLorme: Maine Atlas & Gazetteer:* Map 41; USGS Barren Mountain East

Trail contact: Appalachian Mountain Club, Greenville Office; (207) 695-3085; outdoors.org

Amenities available: None

Maximum grade: 20% grade for 0.1 mile. The trail goes up and down along the stream, with some steps and steep sections.

Cell service: None

Finding the trailhead: From the blinking light in Greenville, drive north on Lily Bay Road. Almost immediately turn right onto Pleasant Street and drive 12.3 miles to the Hedgehog gate. After paying your fee, continue another 1.7 miles to a T intersection. Turn right, staying on the KI Road toward AMC Gorman Lodge for 3.4 miles. Turn right onto Third Mountain Road at the sign for Gorman Lodge and drive 0.8 mile. The trailhead parking is on the left, just before the trail and 0.1 mile before the bridge over Henderson Brook. Trailhead GPS: N45° 28.052' / W69° 18.644'

The Hike

Henderson Brook flows under Third Mountain Road just beyond the trailhead. Upstream from the bridge, the stream meanders through a boggy meadow between dark walls of spruce. Below the bridge the stream turns back on itself, looking more like a weedy pond than moving water. But, as you'll discover once on the trail, it is moving. Henderson Brook looks like a pond because it is backed up behind a ridge of bedrock. It tumbles over the rock in a small waterfall.

The trail follows Henderson Brook as it descends through a narrow canyon. You cross and recross the brook. The steep sides are mossy cliffs in places and broken slopes too steep for trees in others. The floor of the canyon is littered with boulders of every size.

Along Henderson Brook

Waterfall at the head of the gorge

Geologically, Henderson Brook's little canyon is related to nearby Gulf Hagas. The difference is mostly in scale. Where Gulf Hagas is awe-inspiring, something one can speak of only in superlatives, this hike traverses a more-accessible landscape. The eye picks out a moss-draped cliff that seems to droop into the stream, a house-sized boulder perched beside the water that looks like you could push it over, a patch of ferns huddled against the slope where water seeps from the rock.

After the second stream crossing, the trail climbs away from Henderson Brook to an old roadbed. If you're doing an out-and-back hike, this is a good place to turn around. If you're continuing on to the KI Road, follow the roadbed back down to Henderson Brook. You have to find a place to cross—which can be a challenge, especially during high water. Across the stream, it's a short hike to the Appalachian Trail and out to the road and your shuttle.

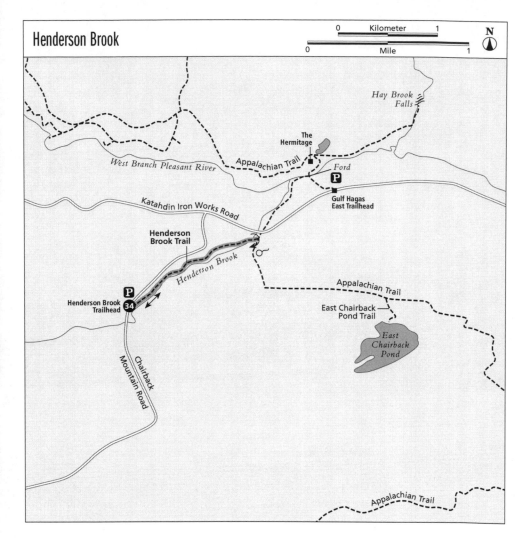

Henderson Brook

Miles and Directions

0.0 Start from the Henderson Brook Trailhead on the east side of Third Mountain Road, between the parking area and the bridge over Henderson Brook.

0.9 The trail follows the stream, crossing twice, to an unaided crossing that may be impassible during high water. If you are hiking the trail as an out-and-back, return the way you came to the trailhead. (*Option:* Continue on the Henderson Brook Trail for 0.1 mile to where it ends at the AT. Turn left and hike 0.1 miles to the KI Road and your shuttle.)

1.8 Arrive back at the trailhead.

35 Chairback Mountain

The hike follows the Appalachian Trail southbound from the Pleasant River to the summit of Chairback Mountain. The hike climbs steeply to a side trail to East Chairback Pond. From there the AT roller-coasters over a series of rocky ridges to an open ridgetop with fine views of the surrounding country and Chairback Mountain. From the ridge, it's a short steep climb to the open cliff tops that are Chairback's summit. The north-facing cliffs offer a spectacular vista.

Start: Gulf Hagas Trailhead, at the west end of the parking area
Distance: 8.2 miles out and back
Elevation gain: 2,425 feet
Hiking time: 5-6 hours
Difficulty: Most challenging
Season: Best May-Oct
Trail surface: Woodland path
Land status: Appalachian Trail
Nearest town: Greenville
Other users: None
Water availability: The first 0.7 mile follows the Pleasant River and then Henderson Brook. There is a spring at 0.9 mile.

Canine compatibility: Dogs must be under control at all times.
Fees and permits: Access fee paid at the Hedgehog gate on the KI Road
Maps: *DeLorme: Maine Atlas & Gazetteer:* Map 42; USGS Barren Mountain East
Trail contact: KI Jo-Mary Forest; (207) 435-6213; northmainewoods.org
 Maine Appalachian Trail Club; matc.org
Amenities available: Outhouse at the trailhead
Maximum grade: 25% grade for 0.3 mile after crossing the KI Road; 14% on the roller-coaster ridge for 0.4 mile; 18% for 0.3 mile to the summit, including a climb up a slide
Cell service: Spotty on the summit

Finding the trailhead: From the blinking light in Greenville, drive north on Lily Bay Road. Almost immediately turn right onto Pleasant Street and drive 12.3 miles to the Hedgehog gate. After paying your fee, continue another 1.7 miles to a T intersection. Turn right, staying on the KI Road toward AMC Gorman Lodge for 4.3 miles. The Gulf Hagas parking area is on the left. The trailhead is at the west end of the parking area. Trailhead GPS: N45° 28.665' / W69° 17.115'

The Hike

The hike follows the Appalachian Trail southbound from the Pleasant River to Chairback Mountain. The trail follows the south bank of the river upstream to Henderson Brook. The AT follows Henderson Brook to the KI Road. Across the KI Road, the trail begins to climb through hardwood forest. You pass a spring near the bottom of the climb.

As you climb, the forest transitions from maple and beech to spruce and hemlock. The trail levels out and slabs east along the ridge above East Chairback Pond. The mountainside drops off sharply to the north. The hardwood forest lower on the slope seems to glow yellow as you hike through deep shade.

Looking northeast from Chairback Mountain's cliffs

Past the side trail to the pond, the AT crosses a series of bedrock folds, the spine of the ridge exposed by erosion of the thin soil. The trail then drops off the ridge and crosses a series of humps that on the topo map look like corduroy swales.

I can remember days when I cursed these irregular folds in the slope. As if a mountain could or should be a smooth, continuous slope from foot to summit. In many ways it's the specifics of a mountain's topography that make it worth climbing. Besides, the work it takes to climb over these wrinkles in the earth's surface sweetens the view from the summit. You appreciate what you earn. Especially on the return hike, when I have to climb out of the narrow notches between the folds, I tell myself that. Over and over until my feet have carried me home.

Finally, the trail emerges onto an open ridgetop with fine views in every direction. Chairback's summit rises vertically across a narrow gap. At the east end of the cliffs is

Chairback Mountain from the trail

a slide that the AT climbs. You are standing on the seat of the chair; the cliff up to the summit forms the chair's back.

From the summit, you can see west, along the face of the Barren-Chairback Range, all way to Big Moose Mountain across Moosehead Lake. Northeast, across the Pleasant River valley, the White Cap Range blocks the view of Katahdin. In the middle distance, Long Pond floats in a deep bowl in front of the Lily Bay Mountains.

Miles and Directions

0.0 Start from the Gulf Hagas East Trailhead, at the west end of the parking area.

0.2 The trail reaches the Pleasant River. Turn left onto the southbound Appalachian Trail.

0.7 Cross the KI Road.

0.8 Pass the Henderson Brook Trail.

0.9 There is a small spring along the trail.

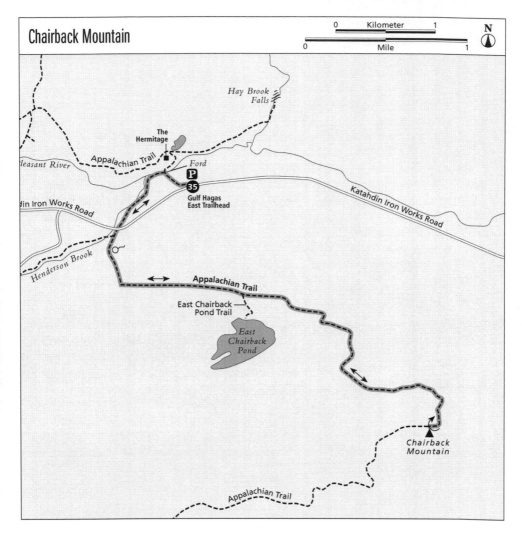

Chairback Mountain

- **1.9** The AT climbs steeply to the top of an unnamed ridge. A side trail descends 0.4 mile to East Chairback Pond.
- **3.2** The AT roller-coasters over several knobs, none with clear views. As you begin climbing in earnest, the AT crosses a small stream.
- **3.6** The AT crosses an open ridgetop with fine views in every direction, including Chairback Mountain's cliffy summit to the south.
- **4.0** Arrive at the base of a slide.
- **4.1** Reach the open cliff tops on Chairback Mountain's summit. To complete the hike, return the way you came.
- **8.2** Arrive back at the trailhead.

36 Third Mountain

Third Mountain is a rocky knob near the center of the Barren-Chairback Range. The Third Mountain Trail climbs gently from the hardwood valley to the rocky evergreen ridge. Once on the ridge, it is a short hike northbound on the Appalachian Trail to Third Mountain's summit and Monument Cliffs, with its fine views north and west.

Start: Third Mountain Trailhead, 200 feet east along Third Mountain Road, on the same side as the parking area

Distance: 4.6 miles out and back

Elevation gain: 1,097 feet

Hiking time: 2–3 hours

Difficulty: Moderate

Season: Best May–Oct

Trail surface: Woodland path

Land status: AMC Recreation and Conservation Area and Appalachian Trail

Nearest towns: Greenville and Brownville

Other users: None

Water availability: The trail follows a small, reliable stream most of the way to the AT.

Canine compatibility: Dogs must be under control at all times.

Fees and permits: Access fee paid at the Hedgehog gate on the KI Road

Maps: *DeLorme: Maine Atlas & Gazetteer:* Map 41; USGS Barren Mountain East

Trail contact: Appalachian Mountain Club, Greenville Office; (207) 695-3085; outdoors.org

Amenities available: None

Maximum grade: 13% grade for 0.3 mile in last climb to the AT; 8% grade for 0.6 mile on the AT to the summit, with a short steep climb in that section

Cell service: Spotty on Monument Cliffs

Finding the trailhead: From the blinking light in Greenville, drive north on Lily Bay Road. Almost immediately turn right onto Pleasant Street and drive 12.3 miles to the Hedgehog gate. After paying your fee, continue another 1.7 miles to a T intersection. Turn right, staying on the KI Road toward AMC Gorman Lodge for 3.4 miles. Turn right onto Third Mountain Road at the sign for Gorman Lodge. Drive 2.1 miles, passing Gorman Lodge Road. The trailhead parking is on the left, just past the trailhead. Trailhead GPS: N45° 27.249' / W69° 18.937'

The Hike

Third Mountain is the middle of five mountains in the Barren-Chairback Range. The range runs roughly east–west south of the Pleasant River and north of the pond-filled flatlands that stretch into the hazy distance.

The hike follows the Third Mountain Trail from the hardwood forest south of Long Pond. You climb gently, following a small stream. The trail only gets steep near the AT, where you climb an exposed bedrock cliff amid mature evergreens. Wooden steps helps with the steepest section.

The northbound AT slabs around Third Mountain, then climbs it from the north. The unmarked summit is a small area of exposed bedrock and stunted pines. You have fine views west and north across the Pleasant River valley.

Long Pond and the Lily Bay Mountains from Monument Cliffs

Looking northeast from Monument Cliffs

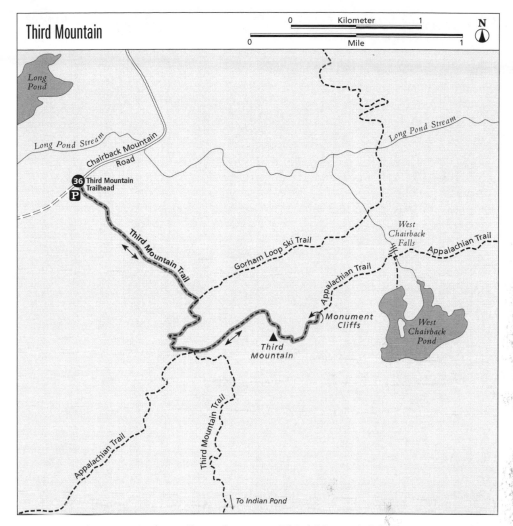

Third Mountain

From the summit, the trail wanders across Third Mountain's ledgy summit ridge to Monument Cliffs. From the cliffs you have open views in every direction except south, which is blocked by Third Mountain.

Miles and Directions

0.0 Start on the Third Mountain Trail, 200 feet east along Third Mountain Road, oMAP: r the same side as the parking area. Turn right, toward the Appalachian Trail.

0.9 The trail climbs gently near a small stream to the Appalachian Trail corridor.

1.4 The trail climbs more steeply to the AT. Turn right onto the AT.

2.0 Arrive at the unmarked summit of Third Mountain.

2.3 The trail wanders across Third Mountain to Monument Cliffs. To compete the hike, retrace your steps to the trailhead.

4.6 Arrive back at the trailhead.

37 Indian Pond

This hike crosses the Barren-Chairback Range on Third Mountain Trail then crosses a wide, flat valley to Indian Pond. There are no views to speak of, but the trail passes through various interesting habitats. You see hanging bogs alight with glowing moss, rocky defiles punctuated by a brook, wide expanses of open hardwood forest carpeted with rocks and wildflower, and the shore of a remote pond.

Start: Third Mountain Trailhead
Elevation gain: 1,678 feet
Distance: 7.4 miles out and back
Hiking time: 4–5 hours
Difficulty: Moderate
Season: May–Nov
Trail surface: Woodland path
Land status: AMC Recreation and Conservation Area
Nearest towns: Brownville and Greenville
Other users: None
Water availability: Much of the hike follows brooks.

Canine compatibility: Dogs must be under control at all times.
Fees and permits: Access fee paid at either the Hedgehog gate (from Greenville) or Katahdin Iron Works (from Brownville)
Maps: *DeLorme: Maine Atlas & Gazetteer:* Map 42; USGS Barren Mountain East
Trail contact: Appalachian Mountain Club, Greenville Office; (207) 695-3085; outdoors.org
Amenities available: None
Maximum grade: 12% grade for the last 0.2 mile to the crossing of the AT; descent from the AT to the valley averages 13.4% for 1.1 miles.
Cell service: None

Finding the trailhead: From the blinking light in Greenville, drive north on Lily Bay Road. Almost immediately turn right onto Pleasant Street and drive 12.3 miles to the Hedgehog gate. After paying your fee, continue another 1.7 miles to a T intersection. Turn right, staying on the KI Road toward AMC Gorman Lodge for 3.4 miles. Turn right onto Third Mountain Road at the sign for Gorman Lodge. Drive 2.1 miles, passing Gorman Lodge Road. The trailhead parking is on the left, just past the trailhead.

From Brownville, drive north on ME 11 for 4.8 miles from the bridge over the Pleasant River. Turn left onto the KI Road at the sign for Katahdin Iron Works and Gulf Hagas. Drive 6.5 miles to the gate, where you pay your fee. Cross the Pleasant River and turn right; drive 3.5 miles to a fork in the road. Take the left fork, following the signs to Gulf Hagas. Pass the Gulf Hagas parking area 2.9 miles beyond the fork. Continue driving another 1 mile. Turn left onto Chairback Road at the sign for Gorham Lodge. Drive 2.1 miles, passing Gorman Lodge Road. The trailhead parking is on the left, just past the trailhead. Trailhead GPS: N45° 27.249' / W69° 18.937'

The Hike

Indian Pond is a large, undeveloped pond on the south side of the Barren-Chairback Range. To get there, you climb on the Third Mountain Trail to the ridge the AT follows. You then cross the AT and climb over the ridgetop. The trail descends gently through a very mossy bog. Past the bog you'll cross a ledge then begin to descend.

Barren Mountain across Indian Pond

The slope is very steep and rocky, but the trail tends to slab to the west rather than descend directly.

You pass a small slide with a partial view south. Descend more steadily, even steeply for short stretches. Along this section, you pick up a tumbling brook to follow. Where the brook reaches the valley floor, widening and quieting, you turn away from it. The trail then seems to wander across the wide valley floor through patches of evergreens and boulders. When the hardwoods are leafless, you get views of Fourth and Barren Mountains along this section.

Several old roads cross the valley floor. The trail uses them here and there. Eventually you end up on a roadbed that seems to be heading straight for Indian Pond, visible through the trees. But the trail turns left and leaves the roadbed. (The road actually never reaches the pond. It turns west before the pond and stays high on the hillside above it.)

The trail stays distant from the pond for 0.5 mile before turning and ending at a campsite on the shore of the pond near its east end. From the campsite, you have a nice view of the pond and Barren Mountain to the west.

This is a remote and little-hiked trail, making it a good place to encounter wildlife, including moose. The valley is covered with wildflowers in spring. Ideally, you

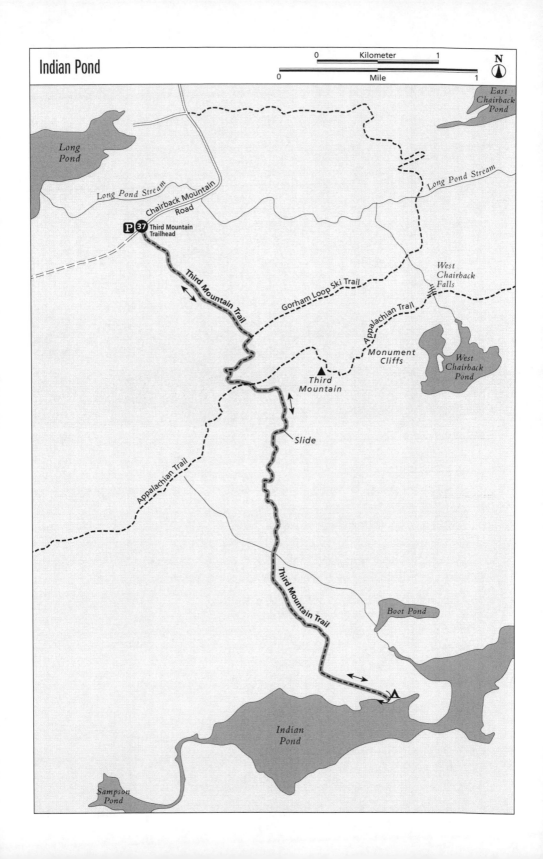

Indian Pond

Looking down the ladder

should hike this trail while the flowers on the forest floor are in bloom but before the trees leaf out.

Miles and Directions

0.0 Start at the Third Mountain Trailhead.

0.9 Climb gently beside a brook. Pass the Gorham Loop Ski Trail.

1.4 Climb more steadily, switchbacking to the AT.

1.5 Cross the AT and climb steeply.

1.7 Descend through a hanging bog to a slide with partial views.

2.3 Descend more steadily beside a brook. As the trail reaches the valley floor, you leave the brook.

3.2 Cross the valley floor. The trail becomes an old roadbed. Turn left onto a yellow-blazed trail.

3.7 Reach a campsite on the shore of Indian Pond. To complete the hike, retrace your steps to the trailhead.

7.4 Arrive back at the trailhead.

38 West Chairback Pond

West Chairback Brook flows out of West Chairback Pond and tumbles off the mountain toward Long Pond. The Appalachian Trail crosses the stream in the middle of that tumble. Upstream from the crossing, the brook drops in an endless chain of very small falls in its bouldery bed. Downstream, the brook crashes down a rock face into a jumble of boulders. The total drop is about 50 feet. West Chairback Pond is a good-sized pond completely surrounded by spruce forest.

Start: Third Mountain Trailhead
Elevation gain: 1,523 feet
Distance: 6.4 miles out and back
Hiking time: 4–5 hours
Difficulty: Strenuous
Season: Late May–Oct
Trail surface: Woodland path
Land status: AMC Maine Woods and Appalachian Trail
Nearest town: Brownville
Other users: None
Water availability: Trail follows a stream in the first 0.5 mile.
Canine compatibility: Dogs must be under control at all times.
Fees and permits: Access fee paid at Katahdin Iron Works

Other maps: *DeLorme: Maine Atlas & Gazetteer:* Map 42; USGS Barren Mountain East
Trail contact: North Maine Woods, Inc.; (207) 435-6213 for road conditions; northwoodsmaine.org; Appalachian Mountain Club, Greenville Office; (207) 695-3085 for trail conditions; outdoors.org
Amenities available: None
Maximum grade: 13% grade for 0.3 mile in last climb to AT; 8% grade for 0.6 mile on the AT to the summit, with a short steep climb in that section. From Monument Cliffs to the saddle between Third and Columbus Mountains the grade is 11% for 0.2 mile.
Cell service: Spotty service on Monument Cliffs

Finding the trailhead: From Brownville, drive north on ME 11 for 4.8 miles from the bridge over the Pleasant River. Turn left onto the KI Road at the sign for Katahdin Iron Works and Gulf Hagas. Drive 6.5 miles to the gate, where you pay your fee. Cross the Pleasant River and turn right; drive 3.5 miles to a fork in the road. Take the left fork, following the signs to Gulf Hagas. Pass the Gulf Hagas parking area 2.9 miles beyond the fork. Continue driving another 1 mile. Turn left onto Long Pond Road at the sign for Gorham Lodge. Drive 2.1 miles, passing Gorman Lodge Road. The trailhead parking is on the left, just past the trailhead. Trailhead GPS: N45° 27.250' / W69° 18.937'

The Hike

West Chairback Pond is nestled into the saddle between Columbus and Third Mountains, surrounded by thick spruce. It's a picturesque lake popular with local anglers. Its outlet stream flows through a marshy area, then drops quickly off the side of the mountain. The Appalachian Trail crosses the stream in the middle of its tumble.

To get there, you have to climb Third Mountain. The trail climbs gently through hardwoods. In spring, this is a great place to see wildflowers. As the climb steepens,

West Chairback Pond

the trees transition to evergreens. A short, rocky climb with one ladder brings you to the AT. Turn left and hike toward Third Mountain.

A rocky climb brings you to the semi-open summit. There are partial views across the valley of the White Cap Range and the Lily Bay Mountains. This isn't the real view, though. Another 0.25 mile of hiking brings you to Monument Cliffs. You get a wide-open panorama of the mountains to the north and west.

Descend off Third Mountain and reach West Chairback Falls. Upstream from the AT, the stream drops chaotically through its boulder-choked bed. It takes a breath at the AT crossing, then leaps off a rock face. Thirty feet down, you can see it flatten out and braid across the forest floor.

To get a good look at the falls from its base, you have to bushwhack down the hillside. The best spots are either about 100 feet west or 100 feet east of the waterfall. The rocky hillside is somewhat overgrown, so even from the bottom you only get incomplete views. To really see the waterfall, you have to boulder hop around the stream near the base.

There's no pool for swimming, but you can take a dip in West Chairback Pond, which is 0.2 mile up a marked side trail. This side trail follows the brook to where it emerges from a marshy area, then turns away from it and ends at the shore of the pond. The pond is irregularly shaped, as if it were trying to find a way to escape the spruce trees that crowd its shore.

West Chairback Falls

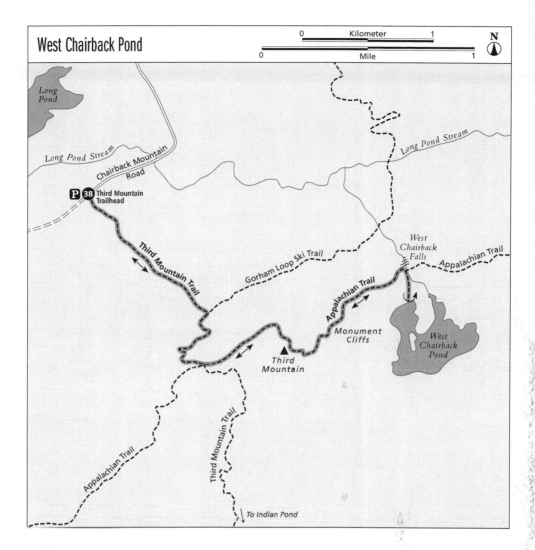

West Chairback Pond

Miles and Directions

0.0 Start at the Third Mountain Trailhead.

0.9 Climb gently to a junction with the Gorham Loop Ski Trail. Continue on the Third Mountain Trail.

1.5 rlimb more steadily; turn left onto the Appalachian Trail.

2.1 Reach Third Mountain's semi-open summit.

2.4 Reach Monument Cliffs.

3.0 Descend to where West Chairback Brook crosses the AT. The falls drop from the rocks you step across.

3.2 Follow the marked side trail upstream to West Chairback Pond. To complete the hike, retrace your steps to the trailhead.

6.4 Arrive back at the trailhead.

39 Barren Mountain

The trail climbs steadily to Barren Slide—a cliff with a large scree slope beneath it. From atop the slide and nearby Barren Ledges, you have fine views east, west, and across Onawa Lake to the south. From Barren Mountain's mostly open summit, you have views in every direction of the surrounding 100 Mile Wilderness and the mountains around Moosehead Lake.

Start: Flagged trailhead at the end of Otter Pond Road

Distance: 6.9 miles out and back

Elevation gain: 2,424 feet

Hiking time: 4–5 hours

Difficulty: Strenuous

Season: Best May–Oct

Trail surface: Woodland path

Land status: Private timberlands and Appalachian Trail

Nearest town: Monson

Other users: Hunters in season

Water availability: None

Canine compatibility: Dogs must be under control at all times.

Fees and permits: No fees or permits required

Maps: *DeLorme: Maine Atlas & Gazetteer:* Maps 41 and 31; USGS Barren Mountain West and East

Trail contact: Maine Appalachian Trail Club; matc.org

Amenities available: None

Maximum grade: Average 19% grade for 0.9 mile on section from junction with the AT to the Barren Slide; last 0.8 mile to the summit averages 17.5% grade, with the final 0.1 mile much steeper.

Cell service: On Barren Slide, Barren Ledges, and the summit

Finding the trailhead: From the blinking light in Monson, drive south on ME 15/6 for 13.8 miles. Turn left onto Elliotsville Road at the sign for Borestone Mountain and drive 7.7 miles. Turn left onto Bodfish Valley Road just after the bridge over Big Wilson Stream. Drive 3 miles, passing the Borestone Mountain Trailhead, to the bridge over Long Pond Stream. Drive another 0.5 mile. Turn left onto Otter Pond Road and continue 0.8 mile to the end of the road. The trailhead is where the roadbed continues straight ahead into the woods; there is flagging to mark the trail. Trailhead GPS: N45° 24.821' / W69° 25.020'

The Hike

Barren Mountain is part of an igneous pluton that rises above the surrounding slate landscape. The rock is of a type that is midway between rough-grained granite and fine-grained basalt. You'll have plenty of time to study the bedrock as you follow the Appalachian Trail up the mountain. But first you have to get to the AT.

The hike follows an abandoned roadbed from the end of Otter Pond Road toward Long Pond Stream. As you make your way across a series of low, swampy areas, you can hear the stream crashing through Slugundy Gorge toward Onawa Lake. Before reaching the stream, the trail turns east and begins climbing a hardwood-covered

The summit from Barren Ledge

ridge. Just past another swampy area, the access trail ends at the AT. Turn right (northbound) on the trail, making note of the place so you can find it on your way back.

The AT climbs over increasingly rocky terrain with partial views of Bodfish Intervale. In the fall the valley and hillsides are a patchwork of bright reds and yellows. In the spring you can find more shades of green than seem possible. The rock beneath your feet is a drab gray, as if the volcanic upheaval that created it cooked the color right out of it.

The view from Barren Slide is one of the most famous in the state. The slide is really a cliff of sharp-edged bedrock with a large scree slope at its base. Take the time to explore along its length and out to the end. On a clear day, it is easy to imagine that you can see all the way across Onawa Lake and Borestone Mountain to the Gulf of Maine. Watch for ravens and raptors soaring on the thermals that rise up along the cliffs. Sometimes moose can be seen in Otter Pond or the swampy end of Onawa Lake.

A short distance farther along the AT, you cross Barren Ledges. Here the rock lacks the corners and angles found on the slide. The cliff is more rounded and granitic, but the view is the same, with the addition of Barren's summit to the east. The remains of the fire tower are clearly visible.

Onawa Lake and Borestone Mountain from Barren Slide

The trail drops off the north side of the ledges and follows a relatively flat ridge toward the summit. The final climb is steep but well-graded, with many steps. At one time, this section of trail had a lot more stonework, including benches. Someone must have decided that benches and stone walkways didn't belong in the wilderness. Now, only enough stonework remains to retard erosion.

The view from Barren Mountain's summit is partially blocked by the encroaching forest, but it includes everything you could see from Barren Slide and all the mountains to the north and east. Slivers of Moosehead Lake are visible between the Lily Bay Mountains and Big Moose Mountain, especially from the steep climb just before the summit. Across the Pleasant River valley, the Whitecap Range blocks the view of Katahdin.

The AT continues northbound past Cloud Pond and its lean-to, then crosses several mountains before descending off the range into the river valley. But those mountains are for other hikes and other days. This time just soak in the raven-high view of the Maine woods before heading back down into the shaley valley to your car.

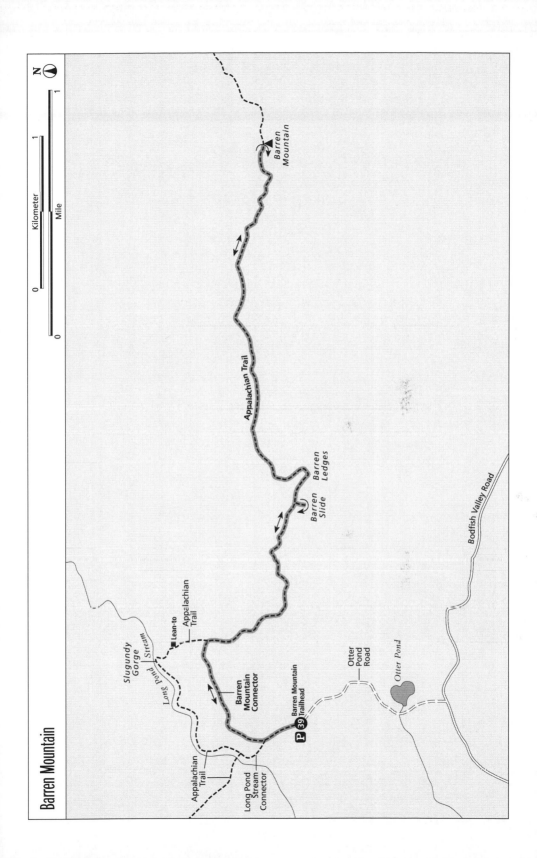

Barren Mountain

N

Kilometer
0 1

Mile
0 1

Appalachian Trail

Barren Mountain

Barren Ledges

Barren Slide

Appalachian Trail

Slugundy Gorge

Long Pond Stream

Lean-to

Appalachian Trail

Barren Mountain Connector

Long Pond Stream Connector

Appalachian Trail

P 39 Barren Mountain Trailhead

Otter Pond Road

Otter Pond

Bodfish Valley Road

Miles and Directions

0.0 Start where the trail enters the woods at the end of Otter Pond Road. The trailhead is marked with flagging.

0.2 The trail follows an old roadbed that is very wet. Stay to the right, where a trail allows you to stay dry. The trail leaves the roadbed and begins to climb.

0.7 Arrive at the Appalachian Trail. Turn right and head northbound on the AT.

1.6 Turn right onto the side trail to Barren Slide.

1.7 The trail descends to the open cliff top with fine views. To continue the hike, return to the AT.

1.8 Turn right onto the AT.

1.9 The trail crosses Barren Ledges with fine views, including Barren Mountain's summit to the east.

3.5 The trail crosses a relatively flat ridge before climbing steeply to the summit. To complete the hike, return the way you came.

6.9 Arrive back at the trailhead.

40 Otter Pond

This hike follows two very short trails from Otter Pond Road to the shore of the pond. It's barely a hike, but the view from the pond is spectacular. Across the pond looms Barren Slide. The pond itself is small and round, with marshy edges—a great place to see wildlife.

Start: Unmarked trailhead across Otter Pond Road from the parking area
Elevation gain: 12 feet
Distance: 0.1 mile
Hiking time: A few minutes
Difficulty: Easy
Season: May–Oct
Trail surface: Woodland path
Land status: Private timberland
Nearest town: Monson
Other users: Hunters in season

Water availability: None
Canine compatibility: Dogs must be under control at all times.
Fees and permits: No fees or permits required
Maps: *DeLorme: Maine Atlas & Gazetteer:* Map 41; USGS Barren Mountain West
Trail contact: None
Amenities available: None
Maximum grade: The hike is essentially flat.
Cell service: None

Finding the trailhead: On ME 15/6, just north of the village of Monson, turn right onto Elliotsville Road at the sign for Borestone Mountain. Drive 7.7 miles and turn left onto Bodfish Valley Road at the sign for Borestone Mountain, just after the bridge over Big Wilson Stream. Drive 3 miles, passing the Borestone Mountain Trailhead, to the bridge over Long Pond Stream. Drive another 0.5 mile. Turn left onto Otter Pond Road and continue 0.2 mile. As you pass Otter Pond, visible through the trees on the right, look for an unmarked parking area on the left. The trailhead is across the road from the parking area. Trailhead GPS: N45° 24.515' / W69° 24.941'

The Hike

Otter Pond is one of those places that most people drive by on their way to other places—in this case the trailhead to Barren Mountain and Slugundy Gorge. Take the time to stop and enjoy this small pond. The trail starts across the road from a parking area (actually, the beginning of an abandoned road). Almost immediately the trail forks. Each trail is about 175 feet long and ends at the shore of the pond. Check both out, since they offer slightly different views.

Barren Slide from Otter Pond

Otter Pond is only a few acres. Around its marshy edges grow sedges and various plants that like to get their feet wet. Naked snags of long-dead spruce trees stick up here and there. On the far shore, a proud spruce grows beside a large boulder. Behind them, the land tilts up to Barren Slide. It's a spectacular view, especially in the fall, when the surrounding forest is awash in reds and oranges.

Don't get completely distracted by the view, though. This pond is a good place to see wildlife, including turtles, ducks, and moose.

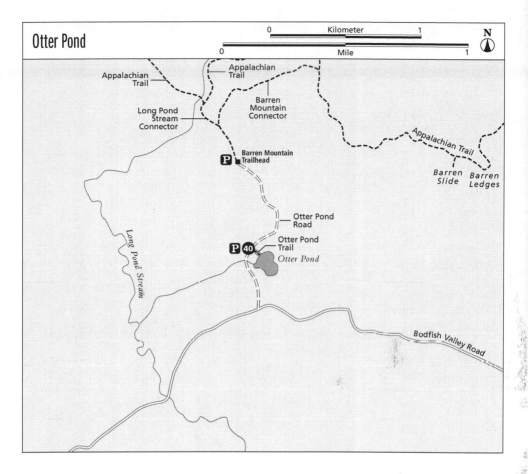

Miles and Directions

0.0 Start at the unmarked trailhead, across Otter Pond Road from the parking area. In 50 feet, the trail forks. The straight-ahead trail leads to the marshy shore of Otter Pond. The right fork leads to a less marshy spot on the shore. Each trail is 175 feet long. To complete the hike, retrace your steps to the trailhead.

0.1 Arrive back at the trailhead.

41 Slugundy Gorge

Long Pond Stream drops more than 200 feet in the short stretch of stream this hike follows. There are no spectacular waterfalls but a nice falls at the head and tail of Slugundy Gorge. This slate gorge is more than 40 feet deep, with nearly vertical sides. Downstream from the gorge is nearly continuous whitewater, with several small drops and pool.

Start: Obvious but unsigned trail at end of Otter Pond Road

Elevation gain: 870 feet

Distance: 3.2 miles out and back

Hiking time: About 3 hours

Difficulty: Moderate

Season: May–Oct

Trail surface: Woodland path

Land status: Private timberland and Appalachian Trail

Nearest town: Monson

Other users: Hunters in season

Water availability: Long Pond Stream

Canine compatibility: Dogs must be under control at all times.

Fees and permits: No fees or permits required

Maps: *DeLorme: Maine Atlas & Gazetteer:* Map 41; USGS West Barren Mountain

Trail contact: None

Amenities available: Hike passes Long Pond Lean-to on the AT.

Maximum grade: Average 16.5% grade for 0.2 mile on the descent from the junction with the AT to Slugundy Gorge

Cell service: None

Finding the trailhead: From downtown Monson on ME 15/6, drive north. As you're leaving the village, turn right onto Elliotsville Road at the sign for Borestone Mountain. Drive 7.7 miles and turn left onto Bodfish Valley Road, just after the bridge over Big Wilson Stream. Drive 3 miles, passing the Borestone Mountain Trailhead, to the bridge over Long Pond Stream. Drive another 0.5 mile. Turn left onto Otter Pond Road and continue 0.8 mile to the end of the road. The trailhead is where the roadbed continues straight ahead into the woods. (The trail isn't the grassy lane to the left.) Trailhead GPS: N45° 24.821' / W69° 25.020'

The Hike

Long Pond Stream flows from Long Pond, nestled against the north side of the Barren-Chairback Range, to Onawa Lake. The stream flows around the west end of the range, dropping 575 feet. About half that descent is in the short section of Long Pond Stream this hike visits. Slugundy Gorge is at the head of the steep section of river.

The trail begins as a continuation of Otter Pond Road. It's often wet, even in summer, but a rough trail that parallels the roadbed allows you to keep your feet dry. Past the wet area, the trail bears right, passes a flagged trail, and begins climbing. You can hear Long Pond Stream; it's only about 0.2 mile through the woods. Climb along a hardwood ridge to the Appalachian Trail. To the right are Barren Ledges and Barren Mountain itself. Turn left (make sure to note the spot, since you'll have to find it

A hiker jumps into the pool below the upper falls.

on your return) and descend toward Long Pond Stream. You pass the side trail to the lean-to, visible through the pines.

The descent steepens. You reach a sharp turn in the trail. Straight ahead is an overlook. Below you is Slugundy Gorge, with a waterfall at its head. It's possible to descend carefully to the stream from this spot, but remember that the rock is slippery; take great care. The stream slides between almost sheer walls 30 feet high. Moss clings to everything. The dark water is more than a dozen feet deep.

The trail descends to Long Pond Stream, where it exits the gorge. There's another waterfall here. For the next 0.5 mile, the Appalachian Trail parallels the stream, which is almost continuous whitewater. There are many small falls and ledges. In several places, the stream has created large pools, good for swimming.

The AT seems to just end at the stream. To continue southbound, you have to ford the knee-deep stream's swift current. There are several good swimming holes near the ford among the jumble of boulders in the streambed.

If you cross Long Pond Stream and continue on the AT, you'll cross Vaughn Brook in another 0.5 mile. The trail fords the brook on a flat slate ledge atop a 20-foot waterfall with a nice pool at its base.

This hike doesn't visit a spectacular waterfall or a single wonderful pool, but the sum total of all the water features is just as satisfying. This is an especially good hike on a hot summer day. Cool air flows downstream with you as you hike. You can walk

Slugundy Gorge

Slugundy Gorge

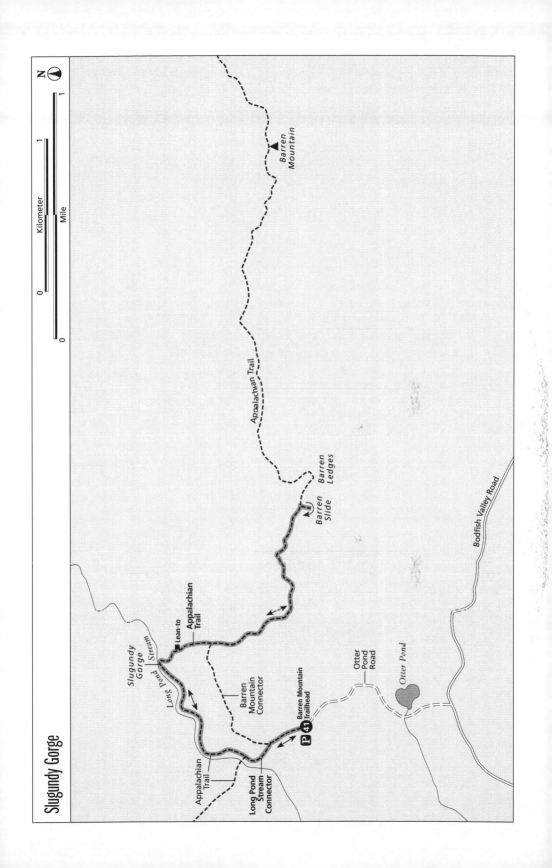

as far as you like or choose a swimming hole in or near Slugundy Gorge itself. You can return by retracing your steps or by following the new-flagged trail from near the AT's ford of Long Pond Stream back to the Barren Mountain Connector. This shortcut saves more than a mile.

Miles and Directions

0.0 Start at the unmarked but obvious Barren Mountain Connector Trailhead.

0.2 Follow an old roadbed through a marshy area. The trail bears right and passes the Long Pond Stream Connector. Begin to climb gently.

0.6 Climb steadily to a marshy area where trail forks; bear left.

0.7 Turn left onto the Appalachian Trail. (**Note:** Remember this spot; since it is unsigned, you'll need to remember where to turn on your return.)

0.8 Pass a side trail to the Long Pond Stream Lean-to.

0.9 Descend steadily to an overlook of Slugundy Gorge and the falls at its head. From this spot, you can climb down—carefully—into the gorge.

1.0 Descend steadily, passing another waterfall at the mouth of the gorge.

1.6 Hike beside Long Pond Stream, passing almost continuous whitewater and several small waterfalls. Reach the point where the Appalachian Trail fords the knee-deep and swift-flowing stream. To complete the hike, retrace your steps to the trailhead. (**Option:** A rough trail is flagged from where the AT crosses Long Pond Stream south to Barren Mountain Connector in 0.3 mile, making the hike a 1.9-mile lollipop.)

3.2 Arrive back at the trailhead.

42 Vaughn Stream Falls

Vaughn Stream and Wilber Brook Falls are pretty waterfalls nestled in the woods east of Monson. The Appalachian Trail crosses each stream at the top of the waterfall. This hike crosses long ridges with few views, but there are interesting slate ledges and lots of wildflowers in the spring.

Start: Parking area where road becomes undrivable
Elevation gain: 1,682 feet
Distance: 6.8 miles out and back
Hiking time: 4-5 hours
Difficulty: Moderate
Season: June-Oct
Trail surface: Old woods road and woodland path
Land status: Appalachian Trail
Nearest town: Monson
Other users: Parking area to AT is a multiuse trail through woods where hunting is permitted in season.

Water availability: Wilber Brook and Vaughn Stream
Canine compatibility: Dogs must be under control at all times.
Fees and permits: No fees or permits required
Maps: *DeLorme: Maine Atlas & Gazetteer:* Map 41; USGS Barren Mountain West
Trail contact: None
Amenities available: None
Maximum grade: 16.6% grade for 0.3 mile descending from ledges; 13.6% descending for 0.6 mile from ridge to Wilber Brook
Cell service: Spotty service on ridgetop

Finding the trailhead: From the center of Monson on ME 15, drive 0.6 mile north. Turn right onto Elliotsville Road at the sign for Borestone Mountain and drive 7.6 miles to the bridge over Big Wilson Stream. Across the bridge, turn left onto Mountain Road at the sign for Borestone Mountain. Drive 0.7 mile uphill across the railroad tracks to the Borestone Mountain parking area. Continue 1 mile and turn left onto a logging road. Drive 0.5 mile and park on the left at the head of a smaller road. The hike begins by following the road down a hill. Trailhead GPS: N45° 23.588' / W69° 26.612'

The Hike

Maine's wildlands—even in the 100 Mile Wilderness—are crisscrossed with old logging roads. This hike takes advantage of one of the roads to access the AT. You follow the road up onto a ridge the AT follows. You head northbound, crossing mossy ledges among big trees. About a mile into the hike, you cross a high ledge with partial views east and south.

You descend off these ledges and sidehill past a large slide in the woods. The trail crosses the base of the slide. You can scramble to the top of the slide for a nice view. Beyond the slide, the trail crosses several small brooks, then descends steadily to an old roadbed. These miles through the woods offer a variety of forest types and therefore

Vaughn Stream Falls

a wide variety of spring wildflowers. Since virtually no one day hikes this section of the AT, most of the year you'll enjoy absolute solitude.

Across the old roadbed, it's a short walk to Wilber Brook. The AT fords the brook on the exposed bedrock at the top of the waterfall. The falls slips between boulders and tumbles into a small pool. You can avoid a wet crossing by bushwhacking upstream about 0.1 mile to where the stream is rockier at the head of an island.

Vaughn Stream is only 0.2 mile past Wilber Brook. Again the AT fords the stream on the rock at the top of the waterfall. Vaughn Stream Falls drops about 20 feet in a single loud plunge. A rough trail heads downstream to the base of the falls. Take time to explore both downstream and up. Downstream, you can get a fine view of the waterfall. Upstream, a large area of boulders in the streambed makes a good lunch spot.

Ledges along the Appalachian Trail

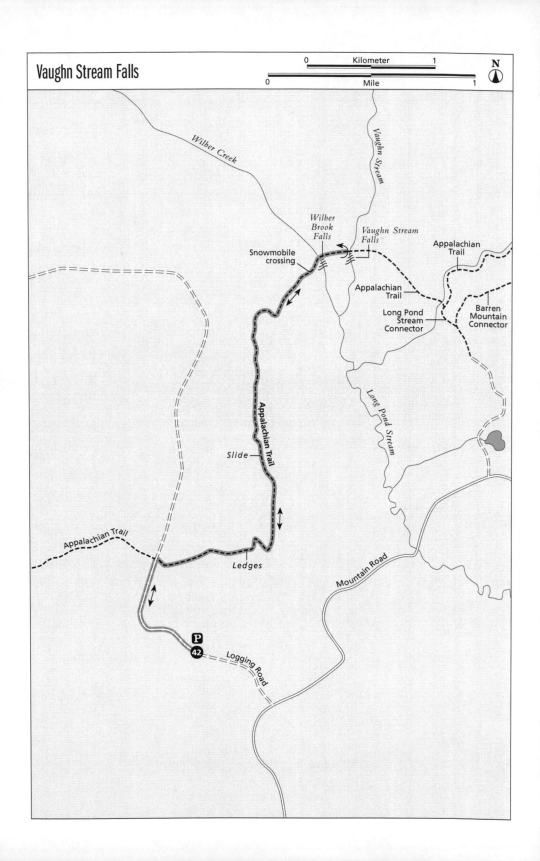

Wilber Brook Falls

Miles and Directions

0.0   Start at the parking area and hike downhill on the road.

0.6   Turn right onto the northbound AT.

1.1   Cross ledges with partial views south and east.

1.9   Descend ledges and hike along the sidehill to a large slide.

3.0   Hike across several small brooks, then descend steadily to an old roadbed. Cross the road.

3.1   Cross Wilber Brook just above a waterfall.

3.3   Reach Vaughn Stream at the top of Vaughn Stream Falls. An unmarked but obvious side trail leads downstream.

3.4   Reach the base of Vaughn Stream Falls. To complete the hike, retrace your steps to the trailhead.

6.8   Arrive back at the trailhead.

43 Big Wilson Cliffs

This hike loops between Big Wilson and Little Wilson Streams, crossing dramatic slate ledges. Most of the ledges are in the woods. The hike is less about vistas and more about the ground beneath your feet. The last set of ledges offers a fine view south and west across Little Wilson Stream's valley. The hike offers options to visit both Thompson Brook Falls and Little Wilson Falls.

Start: Fork in the gravel road to Little Wilson Falls Trailhead
Elevation gain: 1,496 feet
Distance: 6.0-mile loop
Hiking time: 4–5 hours
Difficulty: Moderate
Season: May–Oct
Trail surface: Old woods road and Appalachian Trail
Land status: Elliotsville Plantation and AT corridor
Nearest town: Monson
Other users: Hunters in season
Water availability: Big Wilson Stream
Canine compatibility: Dogs must be under control at all times.

Fees and permits: No fees or permits required
Maps: *DeLorme: Maine Atlas & Gazetteer:* Map 41; USGS Barren Mountain West
Trail contact: None
Amenities available: Outhouse near the trailhead
Maximum grade: Average 8.8% grade for 1.2 miles on climb from Big Wilson Stream to ledges, with short steeper sections. Descent from cliffs to ski trail for 0.1 mile averages 20% grade. Final descent on driveway to trailhead averages 9.7% for 0.3 mile.
Cell service: Spotty service on ledges; strong signal on cliffs

Finding the trailhead: On ME 15/6, just north of the village of Monson, turn right onto Elliotsville Road at the sign for Borestone Mountain. Drive 7.6 miles and turn left onto a gravel road just before the bridge over Big Wilson Stream. Drive 0.3 mile to a fork in the road. Turn right and park on the left. The hike begins by following this road across Little Wilson Stream. Trailhead GPS: N45° 22.447' / W69° 26.575'

The Hike

Big Wilson Cliffs are as unknown as Little Wilson Falls is popular. This hike visits some of the most dramatic slate formations in Maine. The hike starts by following an old road through gravel pits, then follows the road north along Big Wilson Stream. Mostly you can hear but not see the stream. Through the trees on the left, you can see Big Wilson Cliffs. Eventually the road peters out and becomes a trail that ends at the Appalachian Trail.

A short distance northbound on the AT, Thompson Brook flows into Big Wilson Stream from the west. Big Wilson Stream makes an S-bend around slabs of slate bedrock at the junction. It's a pretty spot with a giant pine to sit beneath and enjoy the view. If you're feeling adventurous, cross Thompson Brook and

Big Wilson Cliffs

bushwhack 0.25 mile upstream to Thompson Brook Falls. It's not the most dramatic falls in the region, but it's a pretty series of slides and horsetails that drop about 20 feet altogether.

From Thompson Brook, head southbound on the AT. The trail climbs through mixed forest over increasingly rocky ground, then dramatically up a cleft in a cliff. Atop the cliff, the trail follows the ledges through the woods. The trail follows one ledge then drops down into the woods and climbs another. You do this over and over. All the ledges are slate, but each has its own character. There are no views, only lots of rock and moss. Eventually the trail emerges onto open ledges with dramatic views south and west. The valley beneath you is mostly hardwoods, so the fall colors are spectacular.

The trail drops off the ledges and skirts a small pond, becoming an abandoned road. The southbound AT bears right and crosses the pond's outlet on an old concrete dam. From there it's about 0.5 mile to Little Wilson Falls, if you want to combine the two hikes. If not, follow the road past the pond. The road makes several jogs, passing a couple of camps along the way. Descend a steep drive to the road where you began your hike.

Along the Appalachian Trail

Thompson Brook Falls

Miles and Directions

0.0 Start at the fork and begin hiking north on the gravel road toward Little Wilson Stream.

0.1 Cross Little Wilson Stream on a bridge and past a gated road on the left.

2.0 Follow the road through gravel pits toward Big Wilson Stream. The road bends left and follows Big Wilson Stream. Eventually the road becomes a trail and ends at the AT. Go straight onto the northbound AT.

2.1 Reach Thompson Brook. To continue the hike, retrace your steps to the previous junction. (*Option:* Cross Thompson Brook and then bushwhack 0.25 mile upstream to a slide waterfall.)

2.2 Arrive back at the junction. Bear right, staying on the AT.

2.6 Climb over increasingly rocky terrain to a cleft in the cliffs. Climb to the top and cross ledges in the woods.

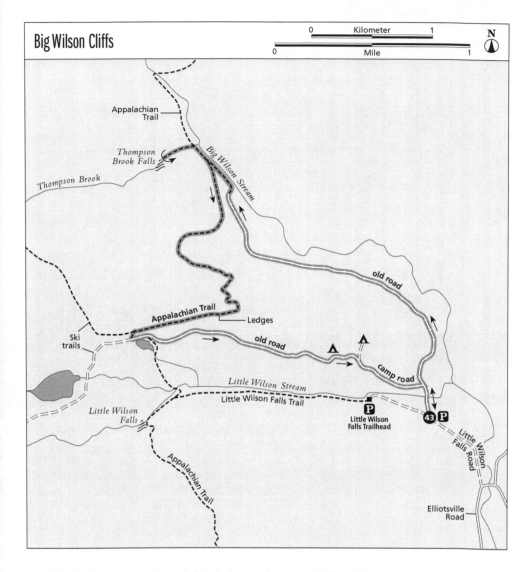

0   Kilometer   1

0   Mile   1

N

3.6 Roller-coaster between ledges in the woods to open ledges with views.

4.2 Descend steadily off ledges to a junction with an old woods road now used as a cross-country ski trail. Turn left, staying on the AT.

4.3 Pass a pond and stay straight on an old road when the AT bears right. (**Option:** Bear right onto the AT and continue 0.5 mile to Little Wilson Falls. Then, using the Little Wilson Falls Trail, you can make this hike a 6.3-mile loop. This is not recommended during high water, as the crossing of Little Wilson Stream is unbridged.)

5.3 Follow the old road past a hunting camp, bearing left then right.

5.4 Turn right, heading downhill.

5.8 Pass a gate across the road. Turn right onto the larger road where you began your hike.

6.0 Cross Little Wilson Stream to arrive back at the trailhead.

44 Little Wilson Falls

At 75 feet, Little Wilson Falls is one of the highest in Maine and the highest on the entire Appalachian Trail. Little Wilson Stream drops from a calm pool into a narrow, black slate gorge overhung with dark cedars. Below the falls, the stream cascades over a series of smaller waterfalls before flowing into Big Wilson Stream. The hike passes several of these falls and offers access to the rest.

Start: End of Little Wilson Falls Road
Distance: 2.5 miles out and back
Elevation gain: 476 feet
Hiking time: About 2 hours
Difficulty: Easy
Season: May–Nov; falls have more water May–early June
Trail surface: Woodland path with lots of roots and rocks
Land status: Elliotsville Plantation and Appalachian Trail
Nearest town: Monson
Other users: None
Water availability: Little Wilson Stream

Canine compatibility: Dogs must be under control at all times.
Fees and permits: No fees or permits required
Maps: *DeLorme: Maine Atlas & Gazetteer:* Map 41; USGS Barren Mountain West
Trail contact: Elliotsville Plantation; (207) 581-9462
Amenities available: None
Maximum grade: Average 4.5% grade for 1.2 miles from trailhead to Little Wilson Falls, with very short steep sections, especially in the last 0.2 mile along the AT
Cell service: Spotty

Finding the trailhead: From the center of Monson on ME 15, drive 0.6 mile north and turn right onto Elliotsville Road (there is a sign for Borestone Mountain just before the turn). Drive 7.6 miles on Elliotsville Road. Just before the bridge over Big Wilson Stream, there is an unmarked gravel road on the left. Turn down Little Wilson Falls Road and drive 0.5 mile to a fork in the road. At the fork go straight and continue another 0.3 mile to the end of the road. The trail leaves the northwest corner of the parking area along the stream. (*Note:* At first the trail looks more like a small, gravelly streambed than a trail.) Trailhead GPS: N45° 22.511' / W69° 26.937'

The Hike

Monson was once the center of Maine's slate industry, the slabs of black rock harvested from several quarries around the town. Until recently, you could see slate stacked, ready to be sold, along the road through town. Many of the streams in this part of Maine cut through slate gorges, drop over slate ledges, or have piles of broken slate along their banks. Nearby Big Wilson Falls—across Elliotsville Road from the dirt road back to the trailhead—is a good example. To the west in Blanchard, the Piscataquis River cuts through a shallow slate gorge below Abbott Road; at the head of the gorge is Barrow's Falls. Northeast of Little Wilson Falls is the most famous slate gorge: Gulf Hagas.

A photographer sets up a shot of Little Wilson Falls.

In most of these cases, the sheets of slate are stood on end. Across Little Wilson Falls from the trail, the cliff shows this vertical bedding. You can see the same thing when you hike Gulf Hagas. Along the trail to Little Wilson Falls, there are several places where fins of slate stick out of the hillside. Near the falls, the top of the gorge has several large fins of slate that jut out into space. The blackness of the slate, the vertical bedding, and the forest closing over the gorge and falls all make Little Wilson Falls the most dramatic waterfall in Maine.

The trail begins at a no-longer-used state campsite. Originally, the trail was a shortcut used by locals to get to the falls. In the summer of 2013, the Maine Appalachian Mountain Club improved and blazed the trail for Elliotsville Plantation, the land's owner. The trail begins along the stream at the large pool below a waterfall and follows the stream up past another good-sized falls. Note that the huge boulder sitting on the slate ledge across the stream is not the same kind of rock: It is an erratic, dropped here by retreating glaciers. Beyond the second falls, the trail begins to gently climb the hillside, staying within earshot and often within view of Little Wilson Stream. The trail turns away from the stream after it levels out atop a ridge, and just before intersecting the Appalachian Trail.

Little Wilson Falls

Along Little Wilson Stream

To reach Little Wilson Falls, turn left and hike southbound on the AT, a rocky and rooty climb up alongside the slate gorge. When you reach the sign-in box just before the falls, there is a place to climb out onto the rocks to see the falls from partway down. Remember as you climb around on the rock that slate is slippery when wet. After exploring the falls, you may want to explore the slate gorge and the stream below the gorge. To do so, pass the Little Wilson Falls Trail and continue northbound on the AT as it drops down to Little Wilson Stream just below the gorge. To get the best view back up the gorge, you need to ford the stream. To explore a horseshoe bend and falls downstream, follow the rough trail on the west bank of Little Wilson Stream for 0.1 mile. When the water is low in late summer, you can cross and recross the stream on the slate at the falls. In the spring, the water rushes over and around the rocks.

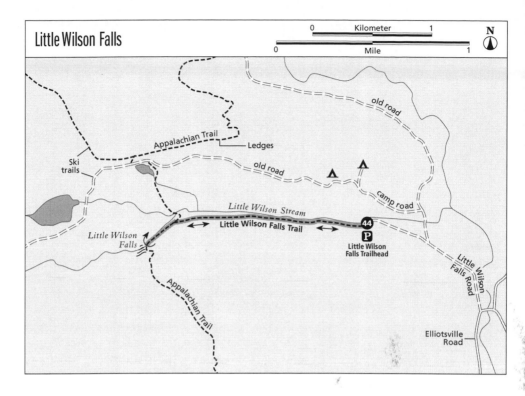

Little Wilson Falls

Miles and Directions

0.0   Start at the northwest corner of the parking area. The unmarked trail looks like a small, rocky streambed that stays close to Little Wilson Stream.

1.1   The trail follows along the stream, passing several waterfalls, then begins to climb. The trail ends at the white-blazed Appalachian Trail. Turn left to hike toward Little Wilson Falls.

1.3   After hiking along the end of the gorge below the falls, arrive at the top of the falls. (**Note:** When climbing around on the rocks, remember that slate is slippery when wet; take care.) To return to the trailhead, retrace your steps.

1.5   Arrive back at the Little Wilson Falls Trail. Turn right to return to the trailhead. (**Option:** Hike straight ahead on the AT, descending to where the trail crosses the stream. This gives you a good view back up the dark gorge and, by bushwhacking downstream 100 yards, access to a horseshoe bend on Little Wilson Stream that is a great place for lunch or just to explore. If you take this option, you'll need to retrace your steps back up to the Little Wilson Falls Trail to get back to the trailhead.)

2.5   Arrive back at the trailhead.

45 Borestone Mountain

The hike to Borestone Mountain is on the Wicked Wild 25 list. The climb to the summits is dramatic and exciting. There's some exposure, but even kids can manage it. The panoramic views are spectacular. It feels like you can see half of Maine. Side trails visit the site of the historic fox farm nestled next to a bog beneath high cliffs and to the Peregrine Cliffs overlook.

Start: Gate across the Borestone Mountain access road
Elevation gain: 1,914 feet
Distance: 5.3 miles out and back
Hiking time: About 4 hours
Difficulty: Moderate
Season: May–Nov
Trail surface: Woodland path and access road
Land status: Maine Audubon's Borestone Mountain Sanctuary
Nearest town: Monson
Other users: None
Water availability: None (in summer they sell water at the visitor center)
Canine compatibility: Dogs not permitted
Fees and permits: Fee paid at visitor center for non-Audubon members

Maps: *DeLorme: Maine Atlas & Gazetteer:* Map 41; USGS Barren Mountain West
Trail contact: Maine Audubon; (207) 781-2330; maineaudubon.org
Amenities available: Outhouse near the trailhead and near the visitor center; museum and gift shop at visitor center
Maximum grade: Average 20% grade for 0.5 mile on climb on Base Trail from the access road, with steeper sections at beginning. Climb from Sunrise Pond to West Peak averages 26% for 0.4 mile, with two much steeper sections. There's a downclimb between the two peaks with a 75% grade for 50 feet.
Cell service: Spotty throughout the hike, with reliable service on peaks and atop Peregrine Ridge

Finding the trailhead: From the center of Monson on ME 15, drive 0.6 mile north. Turn right onto Elliotsville Road at the sign for Borestone Mountain and drive 7.6 miles to the bridge over Big Wilson Stream. Across the bridge, turn left onto Mountain Road at the sign for Borestone Mountain. Drive 0.7 mile up the hill and across the railroad tracks. The parking area is on the left, across the road from the trailhead and Borestone Sanctuary sign. Trailhead GPS: N45° 22.672' / W69° 25.808'

The Hike

Borestone Mountain's name was originally spelled "Boarstone." It seems that from the north, the mountain's rounded, rocky flank rising above Onawa Lake looked like a certain part of a boar's anatomy to the loggers who named the mountain. Sometime early in the twentieth century, the name was changed to the more family—and tourist—friendly "Borestone." The tourists never came, but the new spelling stuck. The valley remains largely undeveloped, and the town at the east end of the lake has been abandoned; nothing is left but a few collapsing buildings.

Looking across Onawa Lake to Barren Mountain from East Peak

The three ponds on the mountain's flank—Sunrise, Midday, and Sunset—were named by the Moore family, who managed a fox farm on the mountain. The Fox Pen Loop Trail you pass on the Summit Trail as you hike around Sunrise Pond winds through the woods among the remains of the pens used to raise the foxes. The fox pelts were shipped to New York City on the nearby Canadian Pacific rail line (you crossed the railroad on Mountain Road as you approached the sanctuary). If you look carefully you can see the high trestle over the southeast corner of Onawa Lake where the railroad passes through the village. The pelts from foxes raised on Borestone Mountain had a reputation for their high quality. They must have drawn consistently high prices, because the Moores hired a well-known architect to design the Adirondack-style lodge on Sunset Pond. The Moore family donated the land to Maine Audubon for the sanctuary. The mile-long Fox Pen Loop Trail is worth checking out on your way down off the mountain.

After hiking up the Base Trail and walking the access road to Sunrise Pond, you need to stop at the visitor center to pay the entrance fee. There is a kid-friendly museum of local flora and fauna at the visitor center, which also sells guides, shirts, and water.

Once around Sunrise Pond, the Summit Trail is fairly steep; the last section before West Peak does have some exposure, but with care it is doable even by small children. The views from the two peaks are well worth the effort. The higher East Peak has

The summit from Peregrine Ridge

two signs on the summit with maps of the mountains you can see all around you. You can see as far west as Sugarloaf and the Bigelow Range; to the east are the flat Penobscot and Piscataquis River valleys, with the hills southeast of Bangor on the horizon. Katahdin would be visible but for the Barren-Chairback Range. In spring, hikers often mistake White Cap's snow-covered summit for Katahdin. To the north are the mountains around Moosehead Lake. This is one of the best views in Maine to enjoy fall colors.

Back at the visitor center, check out the Peregrine Ridge Trail, which begins in the boulders across the parking area from the building. The trail wanders among ledges and boulders before climbing to a cliff-top overlook with a spectacular view of Borestone Mountain across the three ponds.

On your return hike, it is easier to take the access road instead of the Base Trail. The hike is a little shorter, and you pass the Greenwood Overlook. On the hike up the mountain, you passed through forest dominated by evergreens. Along the more gentle south flank of the mountain, the access road passes through beech and especially maple. The maples are tapped each spring.

Miles and Directions

0.0 Start at the gate on the Borestone Mountain access road; 225 feet past the gate, turn left onto the Base Trail.

0.6 Climb steadily, then pass the Little Greenwood Overlook Trail.

0.9 Descend to an access road; turn left onto the road.

1.0 Pass the restrooms, turn left, then wind around to the visitor center on Sunrise Pond. After signing in and paying the fee, continue onto the Summit Trail.

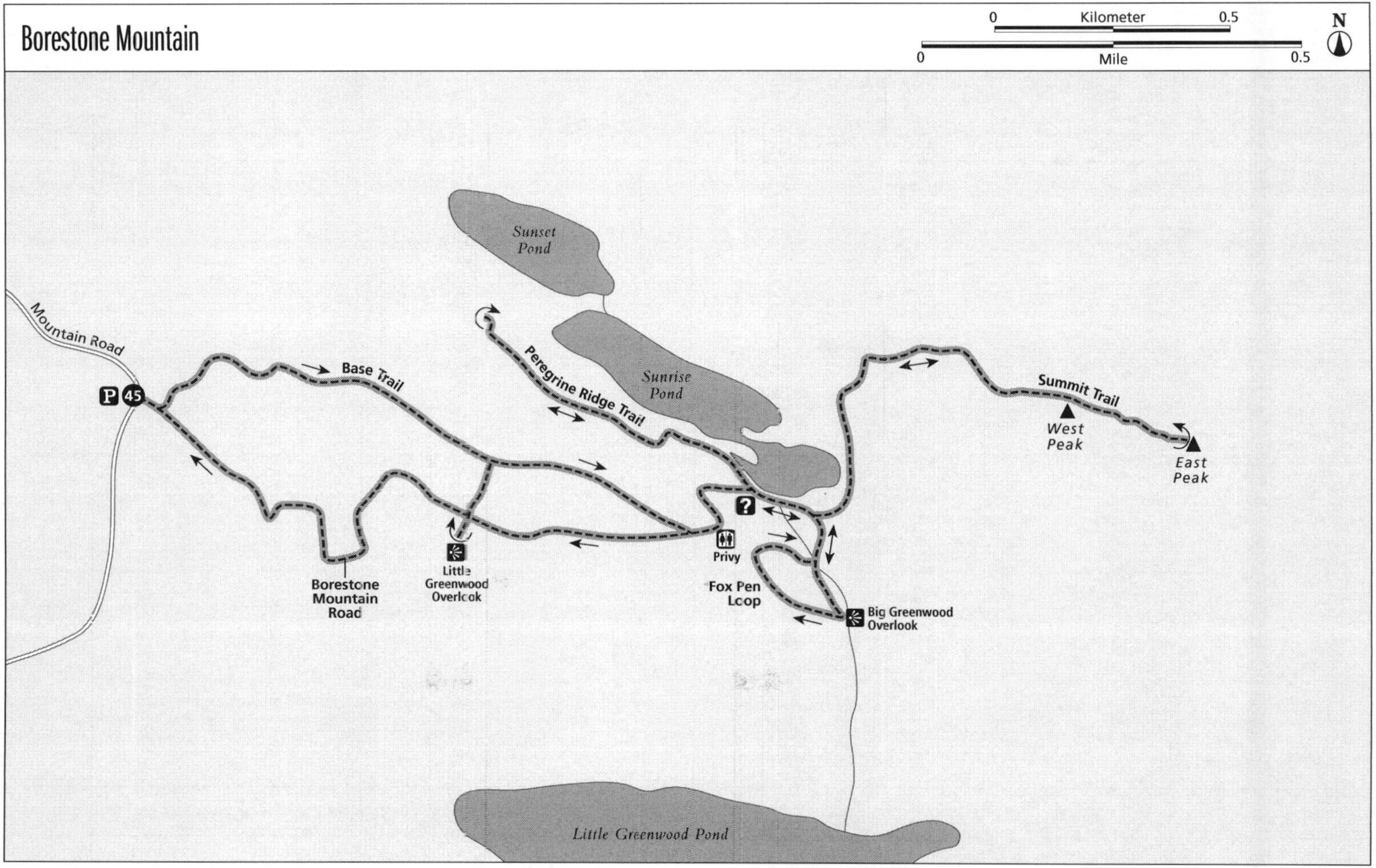

Borestone Mountain

N

Kilometer
0   0.5   0.5

Mile
0   0.5

Summit Trail

East Peak

West Peak

Big Greenwood Overlook

Fox Pen Loop

Privy

?

Sunset Pond

Sunrise Pond

Peregrine Ridge Trail

Little Greenwood Overlook

Base Trail

Borestone Mountain Road

Little Greenwood Pond

Mountain Road

P 45

The steepest section in winter

1.1 Follow the Summit Trail around the pond, passing the Fox Pen Loop.

1.7 Climb steadily then steeply to West Peak.

1.9 Descend steeply off West Peak and climb gently to East Peak. To continue the hike, retrace your steps to the Fox Pen Loop.

2.7 Descend off Borestone's summits and turn left onto the Fox Pen Loop.

2.8 Descend to a bog and cross it on boards. Turn right across the bog.

3.0 Pass old fox pens beneath high cliffs, then turn right onto a short side trail to the Big Greenwood Overlook.

3.1 Past the overlook, complete the loop and turn right.

3.2 Cross the bog and climb to the Summit Trail; turn left.

3.3 Arrive back at the visitor center. Turn right onto the Peregrine Ridge Trail.

3.8 Hike across ledges beside Midday Pond, then climb to the Peregrine Overlook. To continue the hike, retrace your steps to visitor center.

4.3 Arrive back at the visitor center. Turn right on the access road.

4.7 Follow the access road past the Base Trail to the Little Greenwood Overlook. A side trail leads left 200 feet to the overlook atop a large ledge.

5.3 Continue down the access road past the Little Greenwood Overlook and arrive back at the trailhead.

Appendix: Great Circle Trail

The Great Circle Trail was the brainchild of Jay Hall, the regional state forester. The 30-mile loop connects several existing trails with more than a dozen miles of new trail completed in 2021. It's a wonderful backpacking loop. Several of the day hikes in this guide are part of the Great Circle.

There are five road crossings on the Great Circle Trail, so it's possible to hike the loop several different ways. I describe it counterclockwise, starting at the Tumbledown Dick Trailhead near the Turtle Ridge east parking area. Use this as a guide, not a hard-and-fast rule. You can backpack Great Circle in three or four days and from any of the road crossings. How you do it is up to you. For fuller descriptions of each section, check the appropriate day hike. The only section that's not part of a day hike in this guide is the 2 miles along Pollywog Pond.

Some hikers have expanded the Great Circle into a larger loop I call the Greater Circle. Instead of hiking the Appalachian Trail between Nahmakanta Stream Road and Crescent Pond, they follow the Nahmakanta Stream Road east for 1.0 mile to the Debsconeag Backcountry east trailhead. Then they follow the Debsconeag Backcountry Trail to the west trailhead. There are different ways to do this, but the most scenic would be to follow the beginning of the Debsconeag Backcountry, East Loop hike to the ledges above Seventh Debsconeag Pond. From there, turn left and hike the beginning section of the Debsconeag Backcountry, West Loop hike backward to the west trailhead. From there it's a short road walk to the AT. Then follow the AT southbound along Pollywog Gorge to Crescent Pond and reconnect with the Great Circle. This option adds a day of hiking with a campsite at Sixth Debsconeag Pond.

Miles and Directions

The miles are shown for the whole hike with daily totals in parentheses.

Day One

- **0.0** Start at the Tumbledown Dick Trailhead, 300 feet north on Jo-Mary Road from the Turtle Ridge parking area.
- **0.5** Descend gently through hardwood forest to a 0.1-mile side trail to Leavitt Pond. There is a primitive campsite at the pond.
- **0.6** Reach Leavitt Pond on the side trail. To continue the hike, return to the Tumbledown Dick Trail.
- **0.7** Turn right back onto the Tumbledown Dick Trail.
- **2.0** The trail wanders through second-growth forest over low ledges. A short side trail leads to Tumbledown Dick Pond, where there's a primitive campsite.
- **2.1** The trail reaches Tumbledown Dick Stream at the pond's outlet.
- **3.6** Follow Tumbledown Dick Stream. As the stream grows, the trail sidehills up away from the brook then descends gently to a logging road. Turn left onto the logging road.

3.7 Cross a bridge over Tumbledown Dick Stream and immediately turn right, back onto the Tumbledown Dick Trail.

3.8 Follow Tumbledown Dick Stream where it flows between low granite ledges. Reach the top of Tumbledown Dick Falls.

4.0 Descend through boulders. Turn right on a side trail to the base of Tumbledown Dick Falls.

4.1 Descend steeply through boulders to the base of the falls. To continue the hike, return to the Tumbledown Dick Trail.

4.2 Turn right, back on the Tumbledown Dick Trail.

5.1 Descend gently through hardwoods. Turn left (northbound) onto the AT.

6.1 Follow Nahmakanta Stream. Cross Nahmakanta Stream Road.

6.4 Follow Nahmakanta Stream for a short distance, then head through the woods to a boat launch track. Turn right onto the track then left, back onto the AT within sight of the south end of Nahmakanta Lake.

6.8 Reach a small beach near the south end of Nahmakanta Lake.

7.2 Cross a brook.

7.7 Reach another beach.

8.4 Cross a rocky headland, climbing and descending steeply. There's a fine view across the lake from the top of the headland. After descending off the headland, reach a signed 50-foot side trail to a sandy beach with a spring.

8.7 Wander through the woods away from Nahmakanta Lake and cross Wadleigh Brook.

8.9 Reach the Wadleigh Brook Lean-to. End of Day One.

Day Two

9.3 (0.4) Climb steadily to the top of a cliff in the woods.

9.6 (0.7) Climb steadily to ledges with a view.

9.7 (0.8) Climb steadily; pass a giant natural cairn.

10.1 (1.2) Climb through a gorge.

10.6 (1.7) Climb steadily to a grassy saddle between two peaks of Nesuntabunt Mountain.

10.7 (1.8) Climb steadily to the summit of Nesuntabunt Mountain. Go straight onto a side trail to an overlook.

10.8 (1.9) Reach end of the side trail at the Katahdin overlook. To continue the hike, retrace your steps to the AT.

10.9 (2.0) Turn right, back onto the AT.

11.2 (2.3) Descend steeply then slab around cliffs, descending to their base.

11.5 (2.6) A short side trail leads to a ledge overlook.

12.1 (3.2) Descend gently. Cross Wadleigh Pond Road.

12.6 (3.7) Cross a rocky hill. Descend gently to Crescent Pond.

12.8 (3.9) Reach ledges at the east end of Crescent Pond.

13.2 (4.3) Hike around Crescent Pond. Turn left off the AT onto the Great Circle Trail.

13.6 (4.7) Cross Crescent Pond's outlet and descend gently through spruces. Go straight at the junction toward Pollywog Falls.

13.8 (4.9) Turn hard right onto a signed side trail to Lower Pollywog Falls.

14.0 (5.1)   Descend gently then steeply to the base of Lower Pollywog Falls. To continue the hike, retrace your steps to the Great Circle Trail.

14.2 (5.3)   Turn right, back onto the Great Circle Trail.

14.3 (5.4)   Turn right onto the signed side trail to Upper Pollywog Falls.

14.4 (5.5)   Descend gently to granite ledges beside Upper Pollywog Falls. To continue the hike, return to the Great Circle Trail.

14.5 (5.6)   Turn right onto the Great Circle Trail.

14.6 (5.7)   Descend to the end of Pollywog Pond Road.

14.7 (5.8)   Pass parking and a short side trail to a picnic area on Pollywog Pond. Continue up the road. Turn right at the sign onto the Great Circle Trail.

15.3 (6.4)   A short, unmarked trail leads to ledges on the shore of Pollywog Pond.

16.0 (7.1)   Turn right on a short side trail to a campsite on the shore of Pollywog Pond. End of Day Two.

Day Three

16.3 (0.3)   Turn right onto Wadleigh Outlet Road.

16.7 (0.7)   Cross Wadleigh Outlet on a bridge, then turn left off the roadbed onto the Great Circle Trail.

16.8 (0.8)   Follow the north shore of Wadleigh Pond to a lean-to (a tent campsite is 0.1 mile straight ahead along the shore). Turn right and climb steps to the lean-to. Hike past the lean-to and turn left onto the roadbed.

17.1 (1.1)   Turn left off the roadbed and onto the trail.

17.2 (1.2)   Cross Female Brook on very long bridge.

17.9 (1.9)   Begin climbing gently then more steadily beside a small brook. Cross a logging road.

18.4 (2.4)   Climb steadily. Pass through The Gateway.

19.0 (3.0)   Climb steadily then gently through evergreens to Wadleigh Mountain's semi-open summit.

19.2 (3.2)   Descend in steps down ledges to a side trail on the right that leads in 50 feet to upper ledges.

19.3 (3.3)   Descend steeply to marked side trail on the right. Turn right.

19.4 (3.4)   Reach open lower ledges (make sure not to stop at the first ledge with a mostly open view). To continue the hike, return to the Great Circle Trail.

19.5 (3.5)   Go straight onto the Great Circle Trail.

19.7 (3.7)   Slab around the mountain then steeply descend a gully.

20.3 (4.3)   Descend steadily then roller-coaster across the valley floor. Reach an unmarked side trail to Third Musquash Pond.

20.4 (4.4)   Pass a marked side trail that leads to a campsite on Third Musquash Pond.

21.0 (5.0)   The trail follows Musquash Brook, which goes from being wide and marshy to a narrow brook passing through a small gorge. Cross the brook on a bridge.

21.1 (5.1)   The trail follows the brook to the top of a waterfall then turns right, away from the brook.

22.6 (6.6) Wander through woods past some ledges and boulders. Reach a parking area. Cross Penobscot Pond Road. Follow the trail toward Musquash Ledges, turning left 200 feet beyond the road.

22.9 (6.9) Reach Musquash Stream at the base of ledges.

23.3 (7.3) Hike up ledges. Bear left at a junction.

24.0 (8.0) Hike beside Musquash Stream then cross the stream on a bridge.

24.7 (8.7) Climb gently. Turn right onto the Turtle Ridge Trail.

25.1 (9.1) Descend steadily to the shore of Sing Sing Pond.

25.4 (9.4) Turn left, staying on the Turtle Ridge Trail.

25.8 (9.8) Turn left onto a side trail leading to a campsite on the shore of Sing Sing Pond. End of Day Three.

Day Four

26.2 (0.4) Turn right onto the Turtle Ridge Trail from the campsite; turn right again, staying on the Turtle Ridge Trail.

26.9 (1.1) Retrace your steps from yesterday. Pass the trail to Musquash Ledges.

27.6 (1.8) Climb steadily to Turtle Ridge. Roller-coaster on and off the ridge to the first overlook.

27.8 (2.0) Descend then climb to a second overlook.

28.1 (2.3) Descend ledges.

28.2 (2.4) Descend steeply off Turtle Ridge then pass beneath cliffs.

28.5 (2.7) A side trail leads 75 feet to the shore of Hedgehog Pond.

28.6 (2.8) Pass the Hedgehog Cutoff Trail.

29.4 (3.6) Cross Rabbit Pond Outlet on a granite ledge.

29.7 (3.9) Climb onto ledges. Turn left at a junction.

30.1 (4.3) Descend gently through bouldery forest to the Turtle Ridge Trailhead. Turn left onto Jo-Mary Road.

30.2 (4.4) Arrive back at the Turtle Ridge parking area. End of Day Four.

Hike Index

Baker Mountain, 129

Barren Mountain, 190

Big Wilson Cliffs, 208

Borestone Mountain, 218

Chairback Mountain, 175

Debsconeag Backcountry, East Loop, 44

Debsconeag Backcountry, West Loop, 39

Debsconeag Ice Caves, 21

Gauntlet Falls, 110

Great Circle Trail, 223

Gulf Hagas from the East, 165

Gulf Hagas from the West, 158

Hay Brook Falls, 123

Hedgehog Mountain, 141

Henderson Brook, 171

Horserace Pond, 25

Indian Falls, 150

Indian Mountain, 132

Indian Pond, 182

Little Boardman Mountain, 106

Little Lyford Ponds, 154

Little Wilson Falls, 213

Lower Bean Pond and Rainbow
    Deadwaters, 30

Musquash Ledges, 76

Nesuntabunt Mountain from the
    North, 50

Nesuntabunt Mountain from the
    South, 55

Number Four Mountain, 126

Otter Pond, 195

Pollywog Falls and Cliffs, 63

Pollywog Falls and Crescent Pond, 59

Potaywadjo Ridge, 101

Rainbow Stream, 34

Rum Pond Loop, 136

Shaw Mountain, 145

Slugundy Gorge, 198

Third Mountain, 179

Tumbledown Dick Falls via Leavitt
    Pond, 84

Tumbledown Dick Falls via the
    Appalachian Trail, 80

Turtle Ridge from the East, 95

Turtle Ridge from the West, 89

Vaughn Stream Falls, 203

Wadleigh Mountain from the North, 67

Wadleigh Mountain from the South, 71

West Chairback Pond, 186

White Cap Mountain via Logan
    Brook, 115

White Cap Mountain via White
    Brook, 119

THE TEN ESSENTIALS OF HIKING

American Hiking Society

American Hiking Society recommends you pack the "Ten Essentials" every time you head out for a hike. Whether you plan to be gone for a couple of hours or several months, make sure to pack these items. Become familiar with these items and know how to use them.

1. Appropriate Footwear
Happy feet make for pleasant hiking. Think about traction, support, and protection when selecting well-fitting shoes or boots.

2. Navigation
While phones and GPS units are handy, they aren't always reliable in the backcountry; consider carrying a paper map and compass as a backup and know how to use them.

3. Water (and a way to purify it)
As a guideline, plan for half a liter of water per hour in moderate temperatures/terrain. Carry enough water for your trip and know where and how to treat water while you're out on the trail.

4. Food
Pack calorie-dense foods to help fuel your hike, and carry an extra portion in case you are out longer than expected.

5. Rain Gear & Dry-Fast Layers
The weatherman is not always right. Dress in layers to adjust to changing weather and activity levels. Wear moisture-wicking clothes and carry a warm hat.

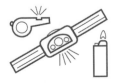

6. Safety Items (light, fire, and a whistle)
Have means to start an emergency fire, signal for help, and see the trail and your map in the dark.

7. First Aid Kit

Supplies to treat illness or injury are only as helpful as your knowledge of how to use them. Take a class to gain the skills needed to administer first aid and CPR.

8. Knife or Multi-Tool

With countless uses, a multi-tool can help with gear repair and first aid.

9. Sun Protection

Sunscreen, sunglasses, and sun-protective clothing should be used in every season regardless of temperature or cloud cover.

10. Shelter

Protection from the elements in the event you are injured or stranded is necessary. A lightweight, inexpensive space blanket is a great option.

Find other helpful resources at AmericanHiking.org/hiking-resources